SCIENCE TECHNOLOGY ENGINEERING MATH

STEM QUEST

FABULOUS
FIGURES
AND
COOL
CALCULATIONS

BARRON'S

First edition for the United States and Canada published in 2018 by Barron's Educational Series, Inc.

Text, design, and illustrations copyright © Carlton Books Limited 2018, an imprint of the Carlton Publishing Group, 20 Mortimer Street, London, W1T 3JW

All inquiries should be addressed to:
Barron's Educational Series, Inc.
250 Wireless Boulevard
Hauppauge, NY 11788
www.barronseduc.com

Executive editor: Selina Wood
Managing art editor: Dani Lurie
Design: Claire Barber
Illustrator: Annika Brandow
Picture research: Steve Behan
Production: Yael Steinitz
Editorial consultant: Jack Challoner

ISBN: 978-1-4380-1135-6

Library of Congress Control Number: 2017959662

Date of Manufacture: May 2018
Printed by Oriental Press, Jebel Ali, Dubai, U.A.E.

987654321

AUTHOR
Colin Stuart

Colin Stuart is a science speaker and author who has talked about the wonders of the universe to well over a quarter of a million people. His books have sold over 100,000 copies worldwide. He is a Fellow of the Royal Astronomical Society and has written articles for the London Mathematical Society and the Institute for Mathematics and its Applications.

For Finley and Ava.

STEM EDITORIAL CONSULTANT
Georgette Yakman

Georgette Yakman is the founding researcher and creator of the integrative STEAM framework with degrees in Integrated STEM Education, Technology, and Fashion Design. She is the CEO of STEAM Education and works in over 20 countries offering educational professional development courses and consulting as an international policy advisor.

ILLUSTRATOR
Annika Brandow

Annika Brandow is an artist specializing in character illustration and illustrated typography. Her work spans advertising, publishing, and online. She loves the challenge of making difficult topics fun and easily digestible through illustration.

The publishers would like to thank the following sources for their kind permission to reproduce the pictures in the book.

9. Art Collection/Alamy Stock Photo, 15. Interfoto/Alamy Stock Photo, 18. Granger/REX/Shutterstock, 23. Bettmann/Getty Images, 33. Universal History Archive/UIG via Getty Images, 36. and 38. Universal History Archive/Universal Images Group/REX/Shutterstock, 43. APA-PictureDesk GmbH/REX/Shutterstock, 44. Shutterstock.com, 49. Pictorial Parade/Hulton Archive/Getty Images, 53. Shutterstock.com, 55. Paul Fearn/Alamy Stock Photo, 56. Public Domain, 57. Alamy Stock Photo, 61. Granger/REX/Shutterstock, 65. Shutterstock.com, 72. Granger/REX/Shutterstock, 73. and 75. Public Domain

Every effort has been made to acknowledge correctly and contact the source and/or copyright holder of each picture, and Carlton Books apologizes for any unintentional errors or omissions, which will be corrected in future editions of this book.

Adult supervision is recommended for all activities.

SCIENCE TECHNOLOGY ENGINEERING MATH

STEM QUEST

FABULOUS FIGURES
AND
COOL CALCULATIONS

Colin Stuart

BARRON'S

CONTENTS

| Numbers & Operations | Measurement | Problem-Solving, Logic & Reasoning | Geometry | Algebra | Advanced Math | Data, Analysis & Probability | Communication |

WELCOME TO STEM QUEST!

We're the **STEM Squad**, and we'd like to introduce you to the wonderful world of STEM: **Science, Technology, Engineering**, and **Math**. The **STEM Quest** series has a book on each of these fascinating subjects, and we are here to guide you through them. STEM learning gives you real-life examples and experiments to help you relate these subjects to the world around you. We hope you will discover that no matter who you are, you can be whatever you want to be: a scientist, an engineer, a technologist, or a mathematician. Let's take a closer look...

SCIENCE

In science you investigate the world around you.

Carlos and **Ella**

Super scientist **Carlos** is an expert on supernovas, gravity, and bacteria. **Ella** is Carlos's lab assistant. Carlos is planning a trip to the Amazon rain forest where Ella can collect, organize, and store data!

TECHNOLOGY

In technology you develop products and gadgets to improve our world.

Lewis and **Violet**

Top techy **Lewis** dreams of being on the first spaceship to Mars. Gadget genius **Violet** was built by Lewis from recycled trash.

ENGINEERING

In engineering you solve problems to create extraordinary structures and machines.

Olive and **Clark**

Olive is an incredible engineer who built her first skyscraper (out of dog biscuits) at the age of three. **Clark** was discovered by Olive on a trip to the pyramids of Giza.

MATH

In math you explore numbers, measurements and shapes.

Sophie and **Pierre**

Math wizard **Sophie** impressed her class by working out the ratio of popcorn-lovers to doughnut-munchers. **Pierre** is Sophie's computer backup. His computer skills are helping to unlock the mystery of prime numbers.

MATHEMATICS IS THE LANGUAGE OF THE UNIVERSE—IT FORMS THE BASIS OF FACTS THAT CAN DESCRIBE ALMOST ANYTHING AROUND US.

Mathematics is a way to count and keep track of changes. Telling time, spending money, counting points, and music are all based on math. The subject is more than just measuring and numbers. Math is about patterns, logic, and shapes, too. It's considered a language that all other languages are based on! Due to this, it is the language that organizes the facts behind other subjects, such as science, technology, and engineering. Some mathematical equations and calculations can rival any painting or sculpture for beauty. And math helps justify the skill of everyday people and engineers to solve problems and to create machines, too. Math can be divided into categories like this:

MEASUREMENT
Finding how much there is of real or imaginery things, distances, and times.

GEOMETRY
The study of shapes and angles.

DATA, ANALYSIS, AND PROBABILITY
Collecting information to look for patterns and trends to help predict what might happen in the future.

NUMBERS AND OPERATIONS
The study of numbers and relationships between them.

PROBLEM-SOLVING, LOGIC, AND REASONING
Figuring out what needs to be studied for understanding inputs, processes, and impacts of choices.

ADVANCED MATH
Statistics, Trigonometry, Calculus, and Theory.

COMMUNICATION
Math is the common organizing language of all other languages.

xy ALGEBRA
Defining math problems in sentences using "shorthand" math operations symbols.

Sometimes people wonder why they need to learn math. They argue that they won't use it in their everyday lives. But you often use math without realizing it—even arguing is using math! This book will show you many ways that math supports our day-to-day existence. Math isn't just about the answers to problems and equations. It is just as much about how you get there. Math teaches you how to tackle problems in logical, clever ways.

The most important part of math problems is figuring out the steps you need to solve them. Math is like the referee of "the game of everyone's life." Math does not lie, it is always what it is. Numbers can be talked about in ways that make them sound good or bad, but when the "facts" are asked for, math is the key to proving ANYTHING!

Let's begin our adventure by figuring out and proving whatever interests us!
Dream big, and good luck!

ADDING AND SUBTRACTING

We use addition and subtraction all the time in our everyday lives to calculate amounts. Let's take a closer look at these simple yet incredibly important calculations.

→ ## what's the BIG idea?

ADDING AND TAKING AWAY

Addition is finding a total when you add two or more quantities of things. If you have 3 bananas and 2 apples, then you have 5 (that's 3 + 2) pieces of fruit in total.

Subtraction is finding out what you have left if you remove some things. If you eat 1 of 4 apples, then you only have 3 (that's 4 − 1) pieces of fruit left.

plus symbol

minus symbol

WHAT'S GOING ON?

SYMBOLS

Humans have been adding and subtracting for thousands of years. But the way we write plus and minus symbols has changed over time. The ancient Egyptians, who lived over 2,000 years ago, had their own symbols (below). The symbols + and − first appeared in a book published in Europe in 1518.

ancient Egyptian symbols for plus and minus

IN FACT...

ANY WHICH WAY

It doesn't matter what order you add things together: 2 + 3 and 3 + 2 both equal 5.

what's the BIG idea?

PLACE VALUE

The value of a **digit** depends on its place in a number. Each place has a value ten times the place to the right. If we want to count higher than nine, we start a new "tens" column to the left. If we want to count higher than 99, we start a new "hundreds" column to the left, and so on.

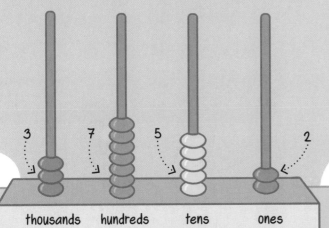

3   7   5   2

thousands   hundreds   tens   ones

WHO WAS RECORDE?

Robert Recorde (1512–1558) was a Welsh mathematician who invented the equal sign =.

COLUMN ADDITION +

You can add numbers with two or more digits together by using column addition. Write the numbers in a column, one below the other. Then add up the numbers in the ones column. If this number is 10 or more, you write the last digit down and add the first digit to the top of the tens column. Then add up all the numbers in that column to get a total.

```
tens ones
  1
  56
+ 27
----
  83
```

AND SUBTRACTION

To subtract numbers using columns in a similar way, put the number you want to take away from at the top. Start with the right (ones) column and take the bottom number away from the top one. If the top number is of lower value than the bottom number, you will to need to borrow a 10 from the left (tens) column, as shown here.

```
 tens ones
      1
  4   5̶6̶
-  2  7
-------
   2  9
```

CALCULATOR SUMS

604

Have you ever noticed that some numbers on a calculator can spell out a word if you turn the calculator upside down?

Complete these sums on a handheld calculator, then flip it upside down to reveal the name of an animal.

$$107 + 282 + 215 = ?$$
$$88 + 161 + 89 = ?$$
$$27432 + 7574 = ?$$
$$199 + 198 + 197 + 139 = ?$$

MULTIPLYING AND DIVIDING

Now that you know how to add and subtract, let's take a look at multiplication and division. Multiplication is repeated addition. Division is splitting into equal parts, or sharing equally.

what's the **BIG** idea?

MULTIPLICATION

Multiplication is really just a quick way to add things up. If you have 5 boxes and they each have 4 chocolate bars in them, then you can calculate the total number of bars by writing $4 + 4 + 4 + 4 + 4 = 20$. But it is quicker to write $5 \times 4 = 20$.

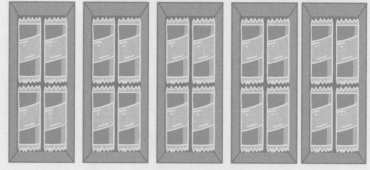

$$5 \times 4 = 20$$

WHAT'S GOING ON?

MULTIPLICATION "X"

The multiplication symbol, x, is often, but not always, used. Sometimes you see · used instead. So $2 \cdot 3 = 6$. And, as we'll see later in the book, when doing **equations** or **algebra** (see p. 70), the x is dropped entirely to avoid confusing it with the letter x. Rather than $2 \times x$, you just write $2x$.

what's the **BIG** idea?

DIVISION

Division is all about calculating how many parts make up a whole. If you take 10 chocolate bars and you want to share them equally among 5 people, then you divide 10 by 5 to figure out how many bars each person gets: $10 \div 5 = 2$.

$$10 \div 5 = 2$$

COLUMN MULTIPLICATION AND DIVISION

To multiply numbers with more than one digit, write the numbers in columns. Say you wanted to multiply 5 x 178. First, multiply the two numbers together: 5 x 8 = 40. Write the 0 in the ones column and carry the 4 over to the top of the tens column.

Next, 5 x 7 = 35. Add the 4 carried over to get 39. Write the 9 in the tens column and carry the 3 over to the top of the hundreds column.

Then, 5 x 1 = 5. Add the 3 carried over to make 8. So, 5 x 178 = 890.

$$\begin{array}{r} {}^{3}{}^{4}178 \\ \times\ 5 \\ \hline 890 \end{array}$$

To divide 578 ÷ 3, write the problem like this:

$$3\overline{)578}$$

3 goes into 5 once remainder 2, so put a 1 above the 5 and carry the 2 to the tens column. 3 goes into 27 nine times, so put 9 above the 7.

3 goes into 8 twice remainder 2, so put a 2 above the 8 and write remainder 2.

So, 578 ÷ 3 = 192 remainder 2.

$$3\overline{)5^{2}78}\ \ 192 \text{ remainder } 2$$

PALINDROMIC MULTIPLICATION

A palindrome is a word that reads the same forward as it does backward—Hannah, Mom, level, and racecar are all good examples. Even sentences can be palindromes. Try "Was it a car or a cat I saw?"

Numbers can also be palindromic. The answers to some of these multiplication problems are palindromes. Can you figure out which ones they are?

143 X 7 = ?
22 X 12 = ?
99 X 21 = ?
407 X 3 = ?
33 X 11 = ?
19 X 5 = ?

POSITIVE AND NEGATIVE NUMBERS

All numbers above zero are positive numbers. For every positive number there is a negative number on the exact opposite side of zero on a number line.

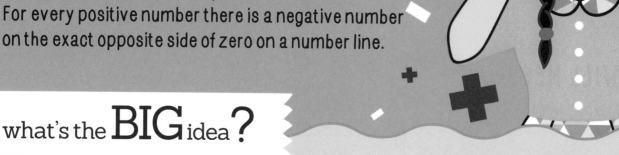

what's the BIG idea?

THE NUMBER LINE

A number line is a helpful way for us to see numbers in order, starting with negative numbers on the left side, moving up through zero, and into positive numbers on the right side.

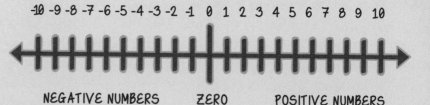

-10 -9 -8 -7 -6 -5 -4 -3 -2 -1 0 1 2 3 4 5 6 7 8 9 10

NEGATIVE NUMBERS   ZERO   POSITIVE NUMBERS

WHAT'S GOING ON?

ZERO

The idea of zero hasn't always been around. Numbers started off as a way to count things when ancient peoples traded goods, such as swapping one animal for three bags of grain. People didn't really need a symbol for zero. Does swapping zero barrels for zero bales of hay make any sense? Not really.

IN FACT...

A PLACEHOLDER

Over 4,000 years ago, people started using zero. At first it was a placeholder to tell the difference between numbers. For instance, a zero helps us tell the difference between 74, 704, and 740. We use a zero as a placeholder when there is no other number needed there.

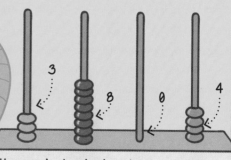

thousands hundreds tens ones

PIRATE TREASURE CHALLENGE

You are a pirate captain looking for a place to bury your treasure. You spot a deserted island. Will it be a safe place to hide your treasure?

YOU WILL NEED:

- ✔ A die
- ✔ One or two buttons to use as counters
- ✔ A pen
- ✔ Paper

IN FACT...
IN THE REAL WORLD

Engineers and other experts consider the height of hills and the depths of lakes and other natural landmarks before installing **phone towers**, or building **dams, reservoirs,** or **wind turbines**.

200
190
180
170
160
150
140
130
120
110
100
90
80
70
60
50
40
30
20
10
0
-10
-20
-30
-40
-50
-60
-70
-80
-90
-100

NEED TO KNOW:

- Sea level is the term used to describe how high something is compared to the level of the sea.

- When you set foot on the shore, you are at 0 ft sea level.

- If you walk into the ocean, your feet will be below sea level, and when you reach 1 ft down, you will be − 1 ft below sea level.

- If you walk onto the land, your feet will be above sea level, and when you reach 1 ft up, you will be + 1 ft above sea level.

INSTRUCTIONS:

POSITIVES—Above Sea Level
LAND: To keep your treasure safe, you should bury it at least 100 ft down. But if you dig down below sea level, you might risk water seeping into your treasure.

Send five scouts out to measure the heights of five nearby hills. For each scout, roll the die three times for each hill. Every dot on the die equals + 10 ft.

(To help you calculate this, each time you roll the die, move your counter along the appropriate number of feet on the number line. Write down your results for the five hills).

When you add up the three numbers for each hill, are any of them more than + 100 ft tall?

NO? Then if you try burying your treasure in the hills, your treasure may get waterlogged.

Yes? Then choose which hill you'd like to bury your treasure in.

NEGATIVES—Below Sea Level
WATER: You send out five scouts to see how deep five coves around the island are. Roll the die three times for each cove to figure out how deep each one is. Each dot on the die is 5 ft, and the ship needs 50 ft of space below the water of a cove so it won't get stuck. How many coves are deep enough for the loaded ship to dock?

(Use the number line to help you.)

Did you manage to bury your treasure and dock your ship? Try the challenge again and see if you get a different result.

PRIME NUMBERS AND POWERS

A prime number is a number that can be divided into whole numbers only by itself and 1. Mathematicians find prime numbers fascinating, and they are always trying to find new ones!

what's the BIG idea?

DIVIDED BY ITSELF

Number 1 is not a prime number because it can only be divided by one number (itself). So the first prime number is 2. It is the only even prime number because all other **even numbers** can be divided by 2.

TRY THIS AT HOME

PRIME NUMBERS UP TO 50

Here's an ancient method called the Sieve of Eratosthenes to help you discover which numbers below 50 are prime numbers.

YOU WILL NEED:

✔ A ruler
✔ A pencil
✔ Colored pencils
✔ Paper

1. Use the ruler and pencil to draw a 10 x 5 grid, like the one on the opposite page.

2. Write in the numbers 1–50.

3. Number 1 isn't prime—color it in red.

4. Start at number 2 (which is prime) and from there, color every second square blue (4, 6, 8, etc). These are all multiples of 2, so they can't be prime.

5. Number 3 is prime, but no multiple of 3 is prime, so color in every third square after 3 in green: 6, 9, etc. (You'll already have colored some in.)

6. The same is true for number 5, so use yellow to color in every fifth square after 5 that isn't already colored in.

7. Color in every seventh square after 7 in brown.

8. Circle any numbers that are left uncolored. These are the prime numbers under 50. There should be fifteen prime numbers in total.

WHO WAS ERATOSTHENES?

Eratosthenes (276 B.C.E.–194 B.C.E.) was an ancient Greek mathematician. Not only did he come up with a way for finding prime numbers, he was also the first person to calculate the distance around the earth (its circumference, see p. 30).

what's the BIG idea?

POWERS

Powers are a mathematical shortcut—a way to save yourself from writing out lots of numbers. Say you wanted to represent $2 \times 2 \times 2 \times 2 \times 2$. You could write 2^5 (said "two to the power five"). These numbers are also called **exponents**.

Here's another example:
$$9 \times 9 \times 9 \times 9 \times 9$$
$$= 9^5$$
or nine to the power five

IN FACT...

MERSENNE PRIMES

A French priest named Marin Mersenne (1588–1648) realized that many prime numbers come in the form of $2^n - 1$ (n represents another whole number). When $n = 74{,}207{,}281$ you get one of the biggest prime numbers known to mathematicians.

$$2^{74{,}207{,}281} - 1 = ?$$

1	2	3	4	5	6	7	8	9	10
11	12	13	14	15	16	17	18	19	20
21	22	23	24	25	26	27	28	29	30
31	32	33	34	35	36	37	38	39	40
41	42	43	44	45	46	47	48	49	50

ANSWERS ARE AT THE BACK OF THE BOOK

FACTORS AND MULTIPLES

As you know, most numbers are made up of other numbers. Factors are numbers you can multiply to get another number. Multiples are numbers you can build when you multiply numbers together.

WHAT'S GOING ON?

PRIME FACTORS

As you've already seen, a prime number is a number that can only be divided by itself and by 1. Factors, on the other hand, are numbers you multiply together to get another number. Any non-prime number has a set of prime factors —factors that are also prime numbers.

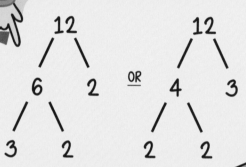

FACTORS OF 12

OR

THE PRIME FACTORS OF 12 ARE 2 AND 3 (12 = 2 X 2 X 3)

what's the BIG idea?

FACTOR TREES

You can find any number's prime factors by drawing a factor tree. The number branches off into the numbers that divide into it. You then find those numbers' factors until you hit a prime number. Always try and divide by two each time, as we know that 2 is already a prime number! Let's look at the factor tree for the number 36:

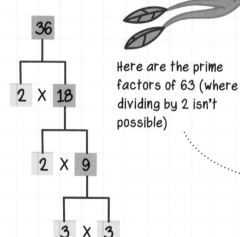

36

2 X 18

2 X 9

3 X 3

So we can say that 36 written in prime factors is 2 x 2 x 3 x 3.

Here are the prime factors of 63 (where dividing by 2 isn't possible)

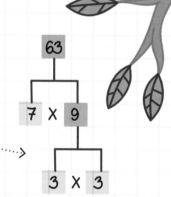

63

7 X 9

3 X 3

63 = 3 x 3 x 7 (always write the numbers in ascending order—from smallest to largest)

MAKE A MOBILE FACTOR TREE

Let's make a colorful mobile based on factor trees. Here's how you do it...

YOU WILL NEED:

- ✔ An adult helper
- ✔ Paper
- ✔ Colored cardstock (or white cardboard you can color in)
- ✔ Colored pencils
- ✔ Round objects of three sizes to trace
- ✔ String
- ✔ Scissors

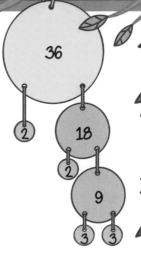

1 Decide what number you would like to make a factor tree for, work out its factors, and write them down on a piece of paper.

2 Trace the large round object onto the cardstock and cut the circle out. Write your number on it with a colored pencil.

3 Trace the medium-sized round object to make circles for your factors. Cut them out, and write the numbers on them.

4 Trace the small round object to make circles for your prime factors. Cut them out, and write the numbers on them.

5 Get an adult to help you punch a small hole at the bottom of the large circle and at the top of the other circles.

6 Thread the string through the holes in the circles in the correct order. Then hang your mobile up!

HIGHEST COMMON FACTOR

If you figure out the prime factors of two numbers, it is also possible to figure out their highest common factor —the highest number that is a factor of both numbers. You simply write down the prime numbers that appear in both lists and multiply them together. The highest common factor of 36 and 63 would be 3 x 3 = 9.

what's the BIG idea?

MULTIPLES

A multiple is what you get when you multiply a number by a whole number (not a fraction, see p. 20). So the multiples of 5 are:

5 (5 x 1), **10** (5 x 2), **15** (5 x 3), **20** (5 x 4), **25** (5 x 5), and so on.

A common multiple is one shared by two or more numbers. For instance, common multiples of 2 and 3 include 6, 12, 18, and 24. You can calculate the Lowest Common Multiple (LCM) of any two numbers from their prime factors. You multiply each prime factor by the maximum number of times it occurs.

Let's go back to 36 and 63. The most times 2 occurs is twice. The most times 3 occurs is twice, and the most times 7 occurs is once. So you write 2 x 2 x 3 x 3 x 7 = 252. Clever, huh?

Now we can see why mathematicians call prime numbers the building blocks of mathematics!

SEQUENCES

A number sequence is a string of numbers that follows a particular pattern. There are lots of beautiful sequences in math to explore!

what's the BIG idea?

THE FIBONACCI SEQUENCE

One of the most famous mathematical sequences is the Fibonacci Sequence. It starts 1, 1, 2, 3, 5, 8, 13, 21, 34, 55... Can you see what the pattern is? To get the next number in the sequence you add the two previous numbers together.

IN FACT...

THE GOLDEN RATIO

If you divide any two neighboring numbers in the Fibonacci sequence, you get a number that approaches 1.618... 21 ÷ 13, for example, is 1.615... and 55 ÷ 34 is 1.618... This number is called the Golden Ratio (see p. 65).

WHAT'S GOING ON?

NUMBER PATTERNS

Let's take a look at some other famous number sequences.

1. TRIANGLE NUMBERS: Can be written as triangles of dots

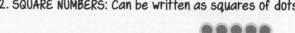

1   3   6   10   15   21, and so on

2. SQUARE NUMBERS: Can be written as squares of dots

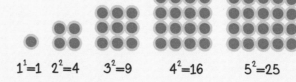

$1^1=1$ $2^2=4$ $3^2=9$ $4^2=16$ $5^2=25$

WHO WAS FIBONACCI?

Leonardo of Pisa (1175–1250)—also known as Fibonacci—was an Italian mathematician. In addition to working on sequences, he introduced the way we write numbers today to Europe.

MUSICAL SEQUENCES

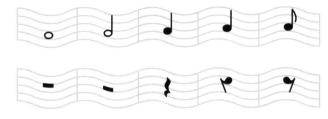

Have you ever noticed that music is made up of sequences? In this activity you and your friends can create sequences made up of different sounds, then put them together to make music!

INSTRUCTIONS:

- Whole note = count to 4
- ½ note = count to 2
- ¼ note = count to 1

Whole				
½				
¼				

Whole				

1. Sing a whole note, counting to four in your head.

Whole				
½				

2. Ask a friend to make a different sound on every 2nd beat for two counts.

Whole				
½				
¼				

3. Add in another sound on every 2nd and 4th beat for one count.

Whole															
½															
¼															

4. Repeat that pattern 3 times and you have a sequence of music!

Now vary the sounds with your friends. You could try bird sounds!

IN FACT...

HOW IS SEQUENCING USED IN THE MUSIC INDUSTRY?

In music recording, each sound (instrument or voice) is recorded on its own track, and then the tracks are blended together using special equipment. Even when musicians play together, they still need to know the timing and sequence of their own parts to get a great end result!

FABULOUS FRACTIONS

Fractions are an easy way to see how something can be divided. Like division and multiplication, fractions show us how many equal parts can make up a whole.

what's the BIG idea?

NUMERATOR AND DENOMINATOR

An example of a fraction is $\frac{1}{2}$. The number on the top of a fraction is called the numerator. The bottom number is called the denominator. Fractions are like division, in that they show us how a whole number can be divided. For instance, $\frac{1}{2}$ of a number or quantity is the same as dividing something by 2. The fraction $\frac{1}{8}$ is the same as dividing one part of something by 8, and so on.

IN FACT...
"TO BREAK"

We get the word "fraction" from the Latin word "fractio," which means to break. Fractions show us how to break up a group into smaller parts. We could say that $\frac{2}{3}$ of your class like chocolate, but $\frac{1}{3}$ prefer ice cream.

$\frac{1}{3}$ like ice cream

$\frac{2}{3}$ like chocolate

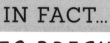

WHAT'S GOING ON?

SIMPLIFYING FRACTIONS

Let's look at how different fractions can be equivalent to each other. If you divided a cake by 6, $\frac{2}{6}$ (2 slices) would be the same amount of the whole as $\frac{1}{3}$. That's because 6 can be divided by 3.

Once you know this, you can simplify fractions. Say you have the fraction $\frac{4}{16}$. You can simplify this fraction by working out which numbers divide into both the top and bottom numbers. For instance, both 4 and 16 can be divided equally by 2 and 4. So you can simplify your fraction like this:

$$\frac{4}{16} = \frac{2}{8} = \frac{1}{4}$$

COMPARING FRACTIONS

Sometimes you'll come across two fractions that have different denominators such as $2/5$ and $3/8$. This makes it tricky to compare the fractions and see which is bigger. Here are steps you need to take to make it easier.

1 Multiply the two denominators together to find the common denominator ($5 \times 8 = 40$).

2 Multiply each numerator by the original denominator from the other fraction to find the new numerators:
($2 \times 8 = 16$) and
($3 \times 5 = 15$).

3 Compare the new fractions
($16/40$ and $15/40$).
Now we can see that
$2/5$ is bigger than $3/8$.

TRY THIS AT HOME

FRACTION MAZE

A lonely alien has been wandering the universe in her UFO. She's turned up lost on Earth and is asking for help to get home. Can you guide her back to her solar system by following the path along which the fractions keep getting bigger?

START $1/4$ $1/2$ $1/8$

$2/16$ $7/8$ $1/3$ $2/5$

$1/6$ $1/3$ $2/7$ $1/5$

$1/10$ $1/2$ $4/5$ $2/10$

$5/16$ $1/16$ $8/9$ FINISH

DIVE INTO DECIMALS

Just like fractions, decimals are a way to show a number that sits part way between two whole numbers. Mathematicians, let's dive into decimals!

→ what's the BIG idea?

THE DECIMAL SYSTEM

Decimals involve divisions of 10. Let's think of the whole numbers 5 and 6 on a number line. There's a gap between them. You can divide that gap up into 10 smaller sections by adding a decimal point, like this: 5.0, 5.1, 5.2, 5.3 up to 5.9. You can also divide the gap between 5.1 and 5.2 into 10 divisions, starting 5.10 up to 5.19.

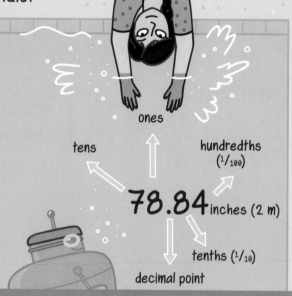

tens   ones   hundredths ($1/100$)

$$78.84\text{ inches (2 m)}$$

tenths ($1/10$)

decimal point

WHAT'S GOING ON?

DECIMAL ARITHMETIC

Decimals can be added and subtracted in exactly the same way as whole numbers:

$$\begin{array}{r} 5.2 \\ +3.7 \\ \hline 8.9 \end{array}$$

You can multiply decimals in a similar way. If there is one number after the decimal point before the multiplication, there will be one afterward. If there are two numbers after the decimal point before the multiplication, there will be two afterward, and so on.

$$\begin{array}{r} 1 \\ 5.2 \\ \times 7 \\ \hline 36.4 \end{array}$$

Multiply by 10, and the number will move one place value to the left. Multiply by 100, and the number will move two place values to the left, and so on.

$$40.6 \times 10 = 406.0$$
$$40.6 \times 100 = 4060.0$$

WHO WAS NAPIER?

John Napier (1550–1617) was a Scottish mathematician who made the use of the decimal point popular.

TRY THIS AT HOME

DECIMALS CARD GAME

0.   0.

In this game you're going to use your ability to figure out which decimal is higher to try and beat your opponent.

YOU WILL NEED:

- ✔ Paper
- ✔ Pens
- ✔ Scissors
- ✔ A pack of cards

1. Cut out two pieces of paper each the same size as a playing card.

2. Write "0." on each piece of paper, and give one to each player.

3. Remove the picture cards from the deck (Kings, Queens, Jacks). You can use the Aces as 1s.

4. Shuffle the deck and deal one card face up to each player next to the 0. paper. Make a note of the card's value.

5. Repeat step 4 going forward. Each time, each player adds up the values of his or her cards. The first player to reach 0.9 gets a point. Write down the scores on a piece of paper. Once a player reaches 0.9, he or she should put his or her cards to the side and start again.

6. If a player draws a 9, they get one point.

7. Keep repeating this until all the cards in the pack have been used. The winner is the person who has the most points.

PERFECT PERCENTAGES

Percentages are another way of showing parts of a whole. They could represent the grade you got on a test, how many people voted in the last election, or the chance of it raining tomorrow.

what's the BIG idea?

"OUT OF" 100

Just as with decimals, the clue is in the name. Percent means per (or "out of") one hundred. If 68% of people go to the movies once a month, that means 68 out of every 100 people.

You can think of a percentage as a fraction of 100.
68% (68 out of 100) as a fraction is $^{68}/_{100}$.
68% as a decimal is 0.68.

100 is divided into 100 equal parts, and 68 out of 100 are shaded

WHAT'S GOING ON?

PERCENTAGE SIGN %

The % symbol represents percent. Take a closer look. It has two zeroes, just like 100, on either side of a /, which means "per." Although you rarely see them, there are symbols for per thousand ($^0/_{00}$) called per mille and per ten thousand ($^0/_{000}$) called per myriad.

what's the BIG idea?

PERCENTAGE INCREASES AND DECREASES

You may encounter percentages in situations where something is increased or decreased. The price of a shirt might be 10% off in a sale or a package of cookies could increase in price by 5%. It is often easier to switch percentages to decimals to do these calculations. For example, if the price of a bike was $100 and it rose by 20%, you'd calculate 100 x 1.20 to get $120.

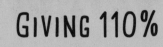

GIVING 110%

Athletes say it all the time—"I gave 110%." You can't really give more than 100% because percent means out of 100. You can, however, have more than a 100% increase in something. For instance, if you increase 70 by 200%, you get 210 (increasing 70 by itself twice).

TRY THIS AT HOME

COUNTING AND GROUPING

Percentages help us compare small groups within larger groups. Let's take a look:

$$\frac{\%}{100} = \frac{is}{of}$$

Often when you are counting objects, they can be split into different types of groups that can be seen as part of the whole group.

If you have 25 things in total and 10 of them can be grouped together, then that represents:

$$\frac{10}{25} = \frac{40}{100} \text{ or } 40\%$$

(There are four 25s in 100, so you multiply 10 by 4.)

If you have more than one type of group out of 100, you can compare them. This **data** equips people with facts when they want to convince other people that things are true (see p. 60).

The total amount of things you count in the big group is the "OF"

The amount of each "type" of thing is the "IS"

100 is the base

YOU WILL NEED:

✔ Paper
✔ A pen

1 Take a look around your house and neighborhood. What types of things can you count out of whole groups?
- Colors of shirts you have
- Types of food in the fridge
- Types of houses you see where you live
- Types of animals you see in nature or pets that people have where you live

2 Make a chart like the one below with different columns for types of groups.

Whole group	How many in the whole group = OF	How many of type A = IS	How many of type B = IS	What % for group A	What % for group B	Which group (A or B) has more?

MEASUREMENT AND ROUNDING

Measuring is an important skill in many areas of life, from weighing out ingredients in cooking to building, science, and finance.

what's the BIG idea?

UNITS

When you write down a measurement, you must always include a **unit of measurement**. Let's say you measure the length of something and you just write down its length as 100. Is it centimeters, miles, or light years? The differences are huge!

	LENGTH =	inch/centimeter	foot/meter	mile/kilometer
	WEIGHT=	ounce/gram	pound/kilogram	ton/tonne
	TIME=	second	minute (60 secs)	hour (60 mins)

METRIC AND IMPERIAL

There are two main systems of units—metric and imperial. The metric system—used by most countries of the world—is based on powers of ten: one hundred centimeters in a meter, one thousand meters in a kilometer, and so on. The imperial system is a much older system that uses units including inches, feet, miles, and pounds.

1 meter is the same distance as 3.28 feet

KILOMETERS

`0 0 0 1 . 0`

1 kilometer is the same distance as 0.6 miles

MILES

`0 0 0 0 . 6`

TRY THIS AT HOME

MASTER MEASURER

Let's practice your measuring skills. See if you can convert from metric to imperial, too!

YOU WILL NEED:

✔ Paper
✔ A pen
✔ A ruler and/or tape measure with both metric and imperial measurements
✔ A helper (optional)

NEED TO KNOW:
Metric to Imperial:
- 1 centimeter (cm) = 0.394 in
- 1 meter (m) = 3.28 ft

1 Write down a list of body parts that you can measure —hand, face, mouth, ear, arm.

2 Use a ruler and measure each body part. Write down the measurements. You may need to get someone to help you measure!

3 Look at both sides of the ruler. Can you figure out what each measurement would be in both the metric and imperial systems?

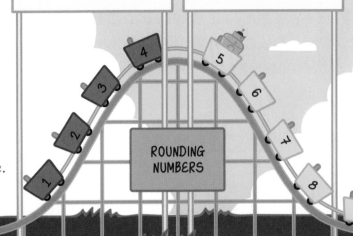

what's the BIG idea?

ROUNDING

Sometimes you don't need to know the exact value of a measurement—something close (an estimate) is good enough. Let's say you weigh something using a super accurate scale and it weighs 7.85772373 lbs. For most purposes, you don't need all those decimal places. You can round the number to one decimal place. To do this, look at the second number after the decimal point. If it is 5 or above, then you add one to the first number after the decimal place. If it is lower than 5, you keep it as it is. So the number above becomes 7.9 lbs to one decimal place.

lower than 5, keep the number as it is

5 or above, round the number up

ROUNDING NUMBERS

TRY THIS AT HOME

ROUNDING BINGO

In this game for two players (or two teams), you'll use your rounding skills to try to defeat your opponent.

Copy this table, one for each player or team. Take turns rolling two dice to form a decimal number. If you roll a 2 and a 1, it would become 2.1. Round it to the nearest half number, and cross that number off the list. The first person to cross out all of his/her boxes wins.

1.0	1.5	2.0	2.5
3.0	3.5	4.0	4.5
5.0	5.5	6.0	6.5

BINGO

MONEY AND INTEREST

Where you put your money can make a difference in how much it grows! Mathematicians, let's take a look at how money and interest work.

what's the BIG idea?

MONEY AND CURRENCY

Money works a bit like fractions, decimals, and percentages in that larger amounts are divided into smaller amounts based on 100. Different countries have their own **currencies** (types of money), but most include bank notes or coins that represent larger values and other smaller coins that represent smaller values. For instance, 100 cents equals 1 dollar ($) and 100 pence equals 1 British pound (£).

TRY THIS AT HOME

PLAYING WITH PENNIES

Can you crack this tricky penny puzzle?

YOU WILL NEED:

✔ Fifteen pennies
✔ Four small money bags

Divide the pennies into the bags so that you could pay for anything that costs between 1 penny and 15 pennies by just handing over the bags (without having to take coins out).

Bag 1   Bag 2   Bag 3   Bag 4

SIMPLE INTEREST

Open a bank account. If you save a certain amount, the bank may give you money. This is called interest, and it is given as a percentage. So you might get 2% extra on your savings. If you put in $100.00 and the bank gave 2% interest after a year, you calculate 100 x 1.02 to get $102.

TRY THIS AT HOME

WANT IT! NEED IT! SAVE FOR IT!

Find out how much money you could save in ten years.

YOU WILL NEED:

✔ A calculator

PUZZLE ZONE

ROBBER RIDDLE

A thief walks into a store and takes a $100 bill from the register without the owner realizing. The thief then uses it to buy $80 worth of stuff, and the owner gives the thief $20 change. How much money did the owner lose in total?

NEED TO KNOW:

You can calculate interest with this calculation:

$$I = P \times R \times T$$

I is the amount of INTEREST earned,
P is the amount put in the bank (or PRINCIPAL),
R is the RATE of interest, and
T is the TIME in number of years.

For example, if you put $100 into a bank account with an interest rate of 3.5% for 5 years, you would earn $100 x 0.035 x 5 = $17.50 interest.
With your calculator, figure out how much interest you could earn if you put $500 into a bank account with an interest rate of 2.5% for 10 years.

GOING IN CIRCLES

The circle is one of the most important shapes in math. Ancient Greek mathematicians thought that the circle was the perfect shape. Let's learn more about circles and see if you agree!

IN FACT...

PARTS OF A CIRCLE

There are many parts to a circle, and they all have their own special names. But perhaps the most important are the diameter—the distance across the circle; the radius—the distance from the center to the edge; and the circumference—the distance all the way around the circle.

Other lines are the chord—a straight line with two endpoints on the circle; the secant line—which goes through two points on a circle; and the tangent—a line that just touches the circle at one point.

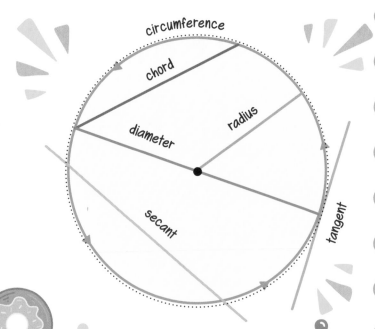

what's the BIG idea?

A SLICE OF PI

There is a special relationship between the radius of a circle and its circumference. Whenever you divide the circumference by twice the radius (or diameter) you always get the same answer: 3.14159... We call this special number pi after the Greek letter π. It doesn't matter whether the circle is the size of a coin or the size of a planet's orbit, the circumference of a circle is always 2 x the radius x π. You can find out more about pi on p. 64.

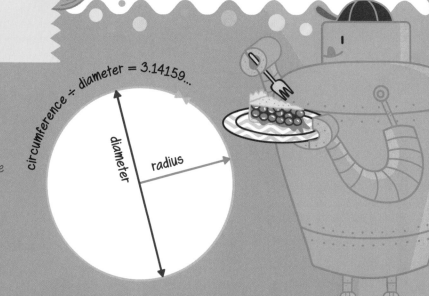

circumference ÷ diameter = 3.14159...

PERFECT PULLEYS

You'll see circles everywhere if you take a look around—in the sun and the moon, flowers, clocks, or even dinner plates. Three-dimensional circle shapes have been featured in important inventions, such as the wheel, gear cogs, and pulleys.

Pulleys are simple mechanisms that people have used throughout history to help lift loads with less effort.

A pulley is a wheel with a rope around it. By pulling down on the rope, you can lift a load. When you combine two pulleys, you can lift an object more easily, with much less effort, because the load is shared by two ropes, as shown—but you have to pull the rope twice the distance.

Pulley mechanisms can be found in machines such as cranes, escalators, and elevators.

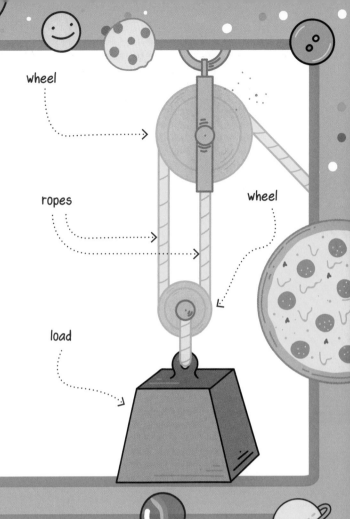

wheel

ropes

wheel

load

HOW TO FIND THE CENTER OF A CIRCLE

Ever wondered how to find the very center of a circle? Here's an easy way to find it.

YOU WILL NEED:

✔ Paper

✔ A pencil

✔ A ruler

✔ A round household object—its diameter should be smaller than the length of your ruler

1 Trace your household object onto the paper to make a circle.

2 Put one end of the ruler on one edge of the circle. Hold the ruler on the edge with one hand while you swing the ruler around with the other hand, measuring across the circle at various points until you find the longest length. When you find the longest length, draw a line across the circle.

3 Repeat step 2 at another (any) point on the edge of the circle, and draw another line across the circle at the longest length. Where the two lines cross is the middle of the circle.

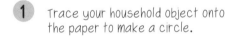

EXPLORING AREAS

Pi isn't just related to the circumference of the circle. You can also use it, together with the radius (R), to figure out the area inside the circle. A circle's area is equal to:

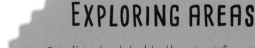

$$\pi \times R \times R \ \text{OR} \ \pi R^2$$

PERIMETER, AREA, AND VOLUME

How do you describe how big something is? Do you say it is large? Mathematicians have an exact way to talk about an object's size. Let's find out how they do it!

→ what's the BIG idea?

1-D, 2-D, 3-D

The perimeter of a shape is the length of all of its sides added together—the total distance around the edge of the shape. This is measured in one-**dimensional** units, such as centimeters. An object's area is the total two-dimensional space inside its perimeter. This is measured in units, such as cm^2 (said "centimeters squared"). Finally, volume is the amount of space taken up by a three-dimensional object. It is measured in units, such as cm^3 (said "centimeters cubed").

7.5 cm

5 cm

Perimeter = 5 cm + 5 cm + 7.5 cm + 7.5 cm = 25 cm

IN FACT...

CHECK OUT THAT NUMBER

You can always tell if a measurement is a perimeter, area, or volume by checking out the power in the units. Just cm (which is really cm^1) is a 1-D (D = dimensional) measurement (perimeter), cm^2 is a 2-D measurement (area), and cm^3 is a 3-D measurement (volume).

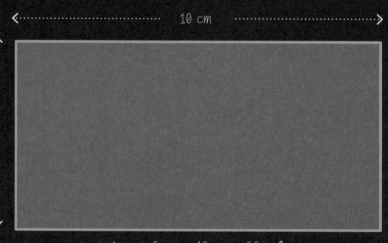

10 cm

5 cm

Area = 5 cm x 10 cm = 50 cm²

HOW TO CALCULATE AREA AND VOLUME

You can use a **formula** to calculate the perimeter, area, or volume of common shapes.

- Perimeter of a square = 4 x one side
- Perimeter of a rectangle = (2 x longest side) + (2 x shortest side)
- Perimeter of a circle = 2π x radius

- Area of square = length of one side^2
- Area of rectangle = shortest side x longest side
- Area of circle = π x radius^2

- Volume of a sphere = 4÷3 x π x radius^3
- Volume of a cube = length of one side^3
- Volume of a rectangular prism = height x width x length
- Volume of a cylinder = π x radius^2 x length

Volume = 5 cm x 2.5 cm x 1 cm = 12.5 cm^3

PUZZLE ZONE

BIRTHDAY CAKE

You have enough icing to cover the edges of a cake with a perimeter of 81 cm. Which shape should you make the cake in order to give you the biggest surface area to put your candles on? A circle, square, or rectangle?

cylinder

PUZZLE ZONE

HOW FAST IS THE EARTH MOVING?

The earth sits 91 million miles (149.6 million km) from the sun. Assuming it has a circular orbit, calculate the perimeter of the circle the earth creates during its orbit. It covers this distance in a year, so how far does it move every hour? (There are 8,766 hours in a year.)

sphere

WHO WAS HIPPOCRATES?

Hippocrates (470 B.C.E.–410 B.C.E.) was an ancient Greek mathematician who was the first to discover that the area of a circle is related to the square of its radius.

ANSWERS ARE AT THE BACK OF THE BOOK

CRAFTY ANGLES

Angles are a measure of turn where two lines meet. They are measured in degrees, which are represented by the symbol °. In a circle, for example, there are 360 degrees (°).

what's the BIG idea?

A CLOSER LOOK...

There are 360° in a full turn, 180° in a half turn, and 90° in a quarter turn (right angle). You can find the size of an angle using an instrument known as a protractor (right). Mathematicians give different names to angles of different sizes, as you'll see below.

340° 350° 0° 10° 20°
330° 30°
320° 40°
310° 50°
300° 60°
290° 70°
280° 80°
270° 90°
260° 100°
250° 110°
240° 120°
230° 130°
220° 140°
210° 150°
200° 190° 180° 170° 160°

WHAT'S GOING ON?

ANGLE TYPES

RIGHT ANGLE
An angle that is exactly 90° is called a right angle.

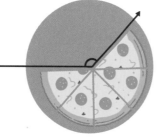

OBTUSE
An angle that is between 90° and 180° is called obtuse.

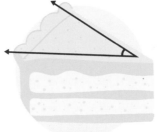

ACUTE
An angle less than 90° is called acute.

REFLEX
An angle that is between 180° and 360° is called reflex.

MAKE A CLINOMETER

How do you measure the height of something far too tall to reach with a tape measure, like a tree or a building? Follow these instructions to make a clinometer—an instrument used in **surveying** and **forestry** to measure heights by using a trick with angles.

YOU WILL NEED:

- ✔ A square sheet of cardstock
- ✔ Tape
- ✔ A straw
- ✔ A weight, such as a washer or wing nut
- ✔ String
- ✔ A skewer
- ✔ A tall object to measure, such as a tree or a building, with plenty of space around it

1 Fold the cardstock in half diagonally to make a triangle. Tape the edges together.

2 Place the straw against the longest side, and tape it in place. You're going to be looking through the straw later so make sure it's not bent or crushed.

3 Hold the cardstock so the right angle is in the bottom left-hand corner. Make a small hole in the cardstock just under the straw above the right angle.

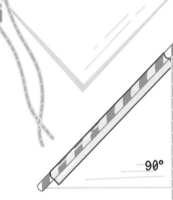

90°

4 Thread the string through the hole, and tie a knot to keep it in place. The string needs to be long enough to dangle a good length past the bottom of the card.

5 Tie the weight to the end of the string.

6 Look through the straw at the opposite end of the hole next to the string until you can see the top of the tall tree or building.

7 Walk toward or away from the object until you can see the object through the straw and the string hangs straight down in line with the edge of the cardstock (right).

8 At this point, the height of the object is now the distance between you and its base (plus your height).

HOW DOES IT WORK?

The triangle you made out of cardstock is an isosceles, right-angled triangle—the two non-right angles are 45° each. When the string hangs straight down, the straw is at a 45° angle so the height of the object and your distance from it are the same.

45°

35

TERRIFIC TRIANGLES

A triangle is a flat, two-dimensional shape with three sides. It is an incredibly stable shape used a lot in building. Mathematicians, if you start looking around you'll soon see triangles everywhere!

what's the BIG idea?

TYPES OF TRIANGLES

Triangles come in four main types based on the lengths of their sides and the angles inside them.

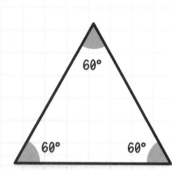

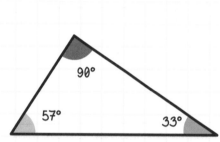

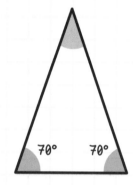

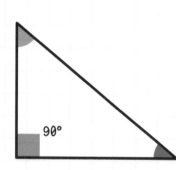

If all three sides of the triangle are the same length, it is called an equilateral triangle. The angles inside an equilateral triangle are identical, too.

Some triangles have all three sides of different lengths, as well as all three angles of different degrees. These are called scalene triangles.

Isosceles triangles have two sides and two inside angles that match.

If one of the three angles inside a triangle is equal to 90°, it is called a right triangle.

IN FACT...

ANGLES IN A TRIANGLE

Triangles get their name because they contain three (tri) angles. Any triangle drawn on a flat sheet of paper will have three angles that add up to 180°.

$$a + b + c = 180°$$

WHO WAS EUCLID?

Euclid (c.350 B.C.E.–c.270 B.C.E.) was an ancient Greek mathematician who wrote about the rules of flat shapes such as triangles. This is called Euclidean **geometry**.

TRICKY TRIANGLES

How many triangles can you spot in this picture?

NOT ALWAYS 180°

The inside angles of a triangle only add up to 180° if the triangle is drawn on a flat surface. Look at this triangle drawn on the surface of the Earth. You can see the angles add up to more than 180°. Triangles on curved surfaces don't obey the rules of Euclidean geometry.

50°

90° 90°

TRY THIS AT HOME

HUNTING FOR
TRIANGLES

Triangles are one of the simplest shapes you can draw, and you'll find them everywhere. You're going to turn into a detective and go searching for triangles!

YOU WILL NEED:

✔ An adult helper

✔ A pencil and paper

✔ Colored pencils

1 Go for a walk with an adult in an area with lots of buildings, such as a town center (or you could walk around your house).

2 Keep your eyes peeled for any triangles.

3 Once you spot one, draw the object in pencil and color in the triangle within it.

4 Write down whether your triangle is equilateral, isosceles, scalene, or right-angled.

PYTHAGOREAN THEOREM AND TRIGONOMETRY

Sometimes you might have information about some angles or lengths of a triangle, but you want to figure out the missing parts. For this you need trigonometry!

→ what's the **BIG** idea?

PYTHAGOREAN THEOREM

The Pythagorean Theorem is all about the sides of right triangles. The longest side of a right triangle is called the hypotenuse. The length of the hypotenuse squared (multiplied by itself) is equal to the sum of the squares of the other two sides.

For instance, $a^2 + b^2 = c^2$ (or $4^2 + 5^2 = 6.4^2$)

If you know the lengths of two sides of a right triangle, you can use the Pythagorean Theorem to calculate the missing length.

WHO WAS PYTHAGORAS?

Pythagoras of Samos (570 B.C.E.–495 B.C.E.) was an ancient Greek mathematician. Strangely, some historians believe he didn't come up with the theory that bears his name!

41
c = 6.4

16
a = 4

b = 5
25

PYTHAGOREAN THEOREM IN PRACTICE

It is easy to see how the Pythagorean Theorem works. Rumor has it that this is how the ancient Egyptians made sure their buildings had perfect right angles thousands of years ago.

YOU WILL NEED:

✔ A long piece of string
✔ A ruler
✔ A marker
✔ Scissors
✔ A friend

WARNING! USE SCISSORS CAREFULLY!

1 Take a piece of string and measure out 24 in (60 cm) with the ruler.

2 Cut the string to this length.

3 Use the marker and the ruler to make dots on the string every 2 in (5 cm).

4 With a friend, make a triangle with the string so that one side is three dots long and another side is four dots long. How many dots are there on the longest side? Did your string triangle prove the Pythagorean to be correct?

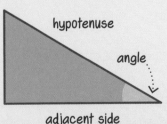

IN FACT...

SIDES OF A TRIANGLE

We know the longest side of a right triangle is called the hypotenuse. Unsurprisingly, the side opposite an angle is known as the opposite side. The side next to an angle is called the adjacent side.

opposite side

hypotenuse

angle

adjacent side

---

what's the **BIG** idea?

TRIGONOMETRY

Trigonometry not only allows you to calculate the lengths of a triangle's sides, it also helps you work out the angles, too.

There are three main trigonometrical functions that allow you to do this. They are called sine (sin), cosine (cos), and tangent (tan). You'll find these on a scientific calculator.

In any right triangle, for any angle:
The sin of the angle = opposite ÷ hypotenuse
The cos of the angle = adjacent ÷ hypotenuse
The tan of the angle = opposite ÷ adjacent

ANSWERS ARE AT THE BACK OF THE BOOK

2-D SHAPES

Mathematicians have a special word for flat, 2-D (two-dimensional) shapes that have straight sides. They call them polygons—from the Greek for "many angles." Let's learn more about these beautiful shapes!

TRIANGLE
(3 sides)

SQUARE
(4 sides)

PENTAGON
(5 sides)

HEXAGON
(6 sides)

HEPTAGON
(7 sides)

→ what's the **BIG** idea?

REGULAR POLYGONS

A regular polygon has sides that are all the same length. That also means all the angles inside a regular polygon are equal. Here are some examples of the simplest regular polygons.

WHAT'S GOING ON?

LINES OF SYMMETRY

A line of symmetry is a line that divides a shape into identical (symmetrical) parts. Here's another way to think about it: if you fold a shape along a line of symmetry, one half of the shape fits exactly onto the other half. A regular polygon has the same number of lines of symmetry as it has sides.

EQUILATERAL TRIANGLE

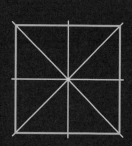

SQUARE

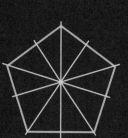

REGULAR PENTAGON

REGULAR HEXAGON

AMAZING ANGLES

In this activity you are going to use a clever trick to figure out the size of the angles in some regular polygons without having to measure them!

YOU WILL NEED:

- ✔ A pencil
- ✔ Paper
- ✔ A ruler
- ✔ A calculator (optional)

1 Use your pencil and ruler to draw a square, a pentagon, and a hexagon. In each shape, pick one corner and use the pencil and ruler to draw a straight line from there to every other corner in the shape. You'll notice this splits the polygon into triangles.

2 We know that the angles in a flat triangle add up to 180°. Because a square contains two triangles, its angles must add up to 360°.

3 There are four angles in a square, which are all equal. If we divide 360° by 4, we can calculate that each angle must be 90°.

4 Use the same idea to figure out how big the angles are in a regular pentagon and hexagon.

5 Can you spot a link between the number of sides a polygon has and the number of triangles it can be split up into? Try it out!

6 How many triangles do you think a dodecagon (twelve sides) can be split into? What about the awesomely named enneacontagon (90 sides)?

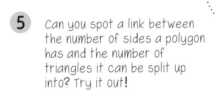

WHO WAS BRAHMAGUPTA?

Brahmagupta (598 c.ε.–668 c.ε.) was an Indian mathematician who worked on a formula (a mathematical rule shown in symbols) related to non-regular quadrilaterals (four-sided polygons).

TESSELLATIONS

Have you ever looked at wallpaper or a carpet and noticed that the patterns are made of shapes that all fit together in a repeating way? Mathematicians call these patterns tessellations.

what's the BIG idea?

REGULAR TESSELLATIONS

The most important thing about tessellations is that they can fill all of a space with no gaps.

There are only three tessellations you can make using the same regular polygons—triangles, squares, and hexagons. If you draw and cut out some regular pentagons, for example, you'll discover that they won't tessellate.

WHAT'S GOING ON?

SEMI-REGULAR TESSELLATIONS

If a regular polygon won't tile space on its own, you can combine it with another to fill in the gaps. These team efforts are called semi-regular tessellations. You can use squares to fill in the gaps between octagons (eight-sided shapes) , for example. There are only seven other semi-regular tessellations.

SEARCHING FOR SEMI-REGULAR TESSELLATIONS

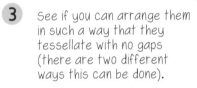

In this activity you're going to see if you can find some of the other seven semi-regular tessellations.

YOU WILL NEED:

✔ A pencil

✔ Paper (different colored paper is best)

✔ A ruler with metric and imperial measurements

✔ Scissors

✔ Colored pencils (if using white paper)

✔ Glue (optional)

1 Draw several squares and regular triangles all with 3 cm sides.

2 Cut them out (and color them in with different colors if you are using white paper).

3 See if you can arrange them in such a way that they tessellate with no gaps (there are two different ways this can be done).

4 If you find an arrangement that works, glue the shapes down to make your own piece of art that you can hang on your wall or the fridge door.

5 If you're feeling adventurous, you can also draw some regular hexagons (6 sides), octagons (8 sides), and dodecagons (12 sides), and try to find the other five semi-regular tessellations.

ANSWERS ARE AT THE BACK OF THE BOOK

IN FACT...

NAMING YOUR TESSELLATION

To name your tessellation, first you need to look at any vertex—a point where several shapes meet. Then count how many of those shapes meet at that point and how many sides that shape has. So, for a tessellation of squares, four squares meet at a vertex and a square has four sides. So this is 4.4.4.4 tessellation. For the square and octagon tessellation, two octagons and a square meet at a vertex, so it is a 4.8.8 tessellation.

WHO IS PENROSE?

Roger Penrose (b. 1931) is a British mathematician who came up with a famous form of tessellation called Penrose tiling (see right).

3-D SHAPES

If a shape has length, width, and depth, it is three dimensional. The most well-known 3-D (three-dimensional) shapes are the sphere and the cube.

what's the **BIG** idea?

PLATONIC SOLIDS

Mathematicians call 3-D shapes polyhedra—which means many bases. There are five special polyhedra. In these, each of its faces is the same 2-D shape (polygon). They are called the Platonic solids and are:

TETRAHEDRON
Four faces

DODECAHEDRON
Twelve faces

ICOSAHEDRON
Twenty faces

CUBE
Six faces

OCTAHEDRON
Eight faces

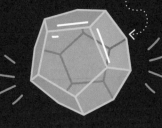

WHAT'S GOING ON?

WHO WAS PLATO?

The Platonic solids are named after Plato (424 B.C.E.–347 B.C.E.), one of the most influential ancient Greek **philosophers**.

THE POWER CONNECTION

We can think of 2-D and 3-D shapes in terms of powers. We know that the area of a two-dimensional shape is measured in units that indicate squaring, for instance cm^2. This small 2 means the same as the power of 2 (see p. 15). With a 3-D shape you can measure the space inside it (or volume) with units written with a small 3 (see p. 32). This is the same as the power of 3.

EYE, EYE!

Having two eyes helps us see in 3-D. If you close one eye and look at a picture and then close the other eye, you'll notice the picture looks slightly different in each eye. Your clever brain merges the two 2-D pictures seen by each eye so you can see it in 3-D, and you can judge how far away things are.

BRAINS, BEWARE!

An optical illusion is seeing an object differently from how it actually is. If the information sent by the eyes is confusing, the brain may take shortcuts and make mistakes, causing the illusion. Optical Art, or Op Art, is even more sneaky! Its artists use certain patterns and colors to create optical illusions. Images on a flat canvas appear to rise up, sink down, or even wiggle.

TRY THIS AT HOME

CREATE YOUR OWN OP ART!

Here's your chance to create some sneaky Op Art of your own!

YOU WILL NEED:

- ✔ White paper
- ✔ A pencil with an eraser
- ✔ A ruler with metric and imperial measurements

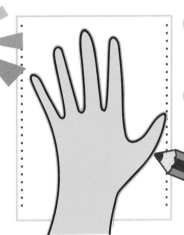

1 Mark dots at 1 cm intervals down both sides of a piece of paper.

2 Trace your hand with a pencil.

3 Use a ruler to draw lines between your dots, but leave the hand area blank.

4 Drawing curved humps, connect the lines over the hand area.

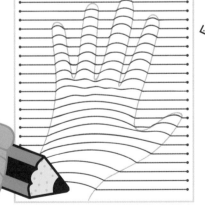

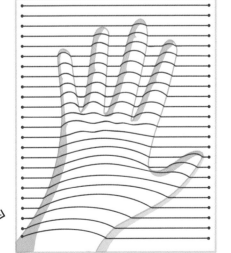

5 Erase the hand outline on one side.

6 Shade along the outline to add depth.

3-D WONDERS

Get to grips with 3-D shapes in all their three-dimensional glory with these incredible projects.

TRY THIS AT HOME

MAKE YOUR OWN PYRAMID

A pyramid is a polyhedron with a flat base and three triangles facing into each other.

The ancient Egyptians built tombs this shape for their pharaohs (kings).

YOU WILL NEED:

- ✔ A pencil
- ✔ A big piece of thin cardstock
- ✔ Glue
- ✔ Scissors
- ✔ A ruler with metric and imperial measurements

1 Use your ruler and pencil to draw a large 3 x 3 square grid on the cardstock. Each square should measure 4 x 4 in (10 x 10 cm).

2 Mark the middle of each side of the square as shown.

3 Draw diagonal lines leading up to the marks as shown. Add an extra line about 1 cm to the outside of the original left-hand lines.

4 Now cut out your folded-out pyramid shape.

5 Fold along the lines as shown.

6 Add glue to the folded tabs, and then stick your pyramid together. How will you decorate it?

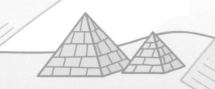

MAKE YOUR OWN CUBE

A cube is a polyhedron with six square faces. It has twelve edges and eight corners.

A die that you use in board games is a classic cube shape.

YOU WILL NEED:

✔ A big piece of thin cardstock

✔ A ruler

✔ Glue

✔ Tape

✔ Scissors

✔ Colored pens

1 Use your pencil and ruler to draw a cross shape out of six 4 x 4 in (10 x 10 cm) squares.

2 Add flaps to the left- and right-hand squares in the cross, leaving the squares going across the cross vertically as shown.

top

3 Cut out the cross shape with scissors, making sure you follow the line of the flaps.

4 Fold the squares in toward each other. Fold the edges of the flap inward.

5 Now add glue to the flaps and stick all six sides of the cube together. Add some tape to make it secure if you like.

6 Decorate it or add dots to each side to turn it into a die!

TRANSFORMATIONS

Have you ever noticed that when you look at an object in the mirror it appears flipped? Reflections are just one way you can change the appearance of a shape. Mathematicians call these changes in an object's appearance transformations.

what's the BIG idea?

TRANSFORMATIONS

Let's take a look at some of the different types.

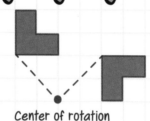

Reflection
A shape is flipped over an imaginary line called the mirror line. A reflected shape is always the same distance from the mirror line as the original.

Center of rotation

Rotation
Rotations occur when a shape is turned through an angle around a point called the center of rotation.

Translation
If you move a shape, but its **orientation** remains the same—it isn't reflected or rotated—you have performed a translation.

WHAT'S GOING ON?

ENLARGEMENT

Another way to transform a shape is to make it bigger. Mathematicians call this enlargement. The scale factor tells you how many times bigger to make the shape.

The other important thing to know is the center of enlargement. A different center of enlargement will put the enlarged shape in a different position. Enlargement is often used when photographs are resized so that the ratio of the sides of the original picture stay the same and the image doesn't become distorted.

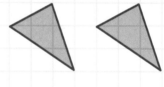

SCALE FACTOR 3
A'B' = 3 × AB
A'C' = 3 × AC
B'C' = 3 × BC

The center of enlargement is 0. The large triangle is 3 times bigger than the small one.

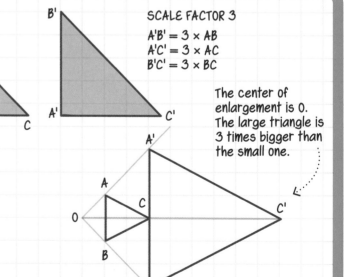

TANGRAMS

A tangram is an ancient Chinese geometry puzzle made of seven different-shaped pieces. Why not create your own and see what shapes you can make by flipping the shapes (reflecting them) and rotating them? Or you could search online for a free tangrams puzzle.

YOU WILL NEED:

- ✔ Paper (it can be colored)
- ✔ Scissors
- ✔ Colored pencils (optional)

CONGRUENT SHAPES

Two shapes are said to be congruent if they are identical in size and shape, even if they are rotations or reflections of each other. Can you find three pairs of shapes in the group below that are congruent?

WHO WAS NOETHER?

Emmy Noether (1882–1935) was a German mathematician who showed that the law of **physics** remain the same even if space is rotated.

RATIOS

We use ratios in our daily lives all the time, such as whenever we bake a cake or run a bath.

what's the BIG idea?

MAKING COMPARISONS

Ratios are all about comparing the size of one part of a whole to another. You might say that the ratio of eight-year-olds to nine-year-olds in a room is 6:4. That means for every six eight-year-olds there are four nine-year-olds. Another way of saying it is that 60% of people in the room are eight years old and 40% are nine years old.

6   4

IN FACT...

YOUR TV

The screen on a TV is a particular ratio. The width of the screen compared to the height is called the aspect ratio. Older TVs are 4:3, whereas more modern widescreen TVs and computer screens are 16:9.

$16 \times \text{height} \div 9$

$9 \times \text{width} \div 16$

WHAT'S GOING ON?

MAPS

One place you're sure to find a ratio is on a map. To represent a town or city on a map, you have to shrink it down to fit on the page. This is done by converting every mile or kilometer into a smaller measurement, such as a centimeter or an inch. The scale of the map might be 1:63,360. That means 1 inch on the map is equal to 63,360 in (or 1 mile) in the real world.

0   1   2
mile

Scale 1:63,360
1 in to 1 mile

IN FACT...

REMEMBER PI?

Pi is a ratio of the diameter of a circle to its circumference. That's $\pi = c{:}d$ (see p. 30).

TRY THIS AT HOME

CRISPY
RICE RATIOS

This has to be the most delicious "Try This At Home" in the book! You're going to use ratios to bake your very own chocolate crispy snacks.

YOU WILL NEED:

- ✔ An adult helper
- ✔ A big bar of chocolate
- ✔ A box of crispy rice-style cereal (or cornflakes)
- ✔ Cupcake liners
- ✔ A stove
- ✔ A weighing scale
- ✔ A pot
- ✔ A heat-safe bowl
- ✔ Water

WARNING! HEAT!

1 These yummy treats are made using a 4:3 ratio of chocolate to cereal.

2 Calculate the weight of cereal you need for the chocolate you have (check the weight on the chocolate wrapper). Weigh the cereal on a scale.

3 With adult help, heat the water in the pot until it is just simmering.

4 Break the chocolate into pieces. Put it into the heat-safe bowl and melt it over the pot of water.

5 Remove bowl from the heat, and stir the chocolate into the cereal.

6 Divide the mixture equally between your cupcake liners and put them in the fridge for at least an hour.

COORDINATES

Coordinates are a set of values that locate a particular point. In math, they can be plotted on a grid with "x" and "y" lines.

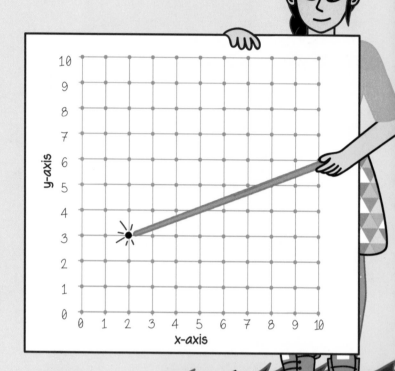

what's the BIG idea?

X AND Y

Take a look at the grid (right). It is divided into sections both horizontally and vertically. The horizontal line is the x-axis, and the vertical line the y-axis. To give the coordinates of the dot, you write down how far it is along the x-axis and how far it is up the y-axis. On this grid, the coordinate is (2,3).

WHAT'S GOING ON?

QUADRANTS

Both the x-axis and the y-axis can extend into negative numbers. This divides the grid into four sections known as quadrants. They are numbered with **Roman numerals** I, II, III, and IV, starting top right and working around counterclockwise (the opposite direction in which the hands of a clock rotate).

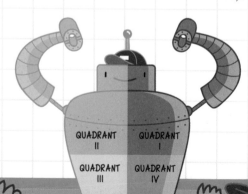

THE THIRD DIMENSION

Coordinates work in three dimensions, too, but you also have to include a third coordinate showing where the point is located on a third axis called the z-axis. These 3-D coordinates take the form (x, y, z).

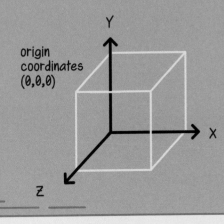

origin coordinates (0,0,0)

WHO WAS DESCARTES?

René Descartes (1596—1650) was a French mathematician and philosopher who invented coordinates. They are named Cartesian coordinates after him.

PUZZLE ZONE

HUNT FOR THE DINOSAUR EGG

A mother dinosaur has forgotten where she buried one of her eggs. It is at the end of the path that doesn't bump into another dinosaur. Where is it hidden? Choose the correct coordinates below to find it!

1. (0,1) (2,3) (1,4) (0,5) (1,7)
2. (3,4) (5,5) (7,6) (9,5) (6,5)
3. (1,1) (2,4) (4,3) (6,1) (9,2)
4. (0,2) (3,4) (4,4) (5,3) (10,3)

ANSWERS ARE AT THE BACK OF THE BOOK

CHARTS AND GRAPHS

A big list of numbers can look endless. Mathematicians use charts to make information and data clearer and easier to understand. Graphs that are used to explain information are called infographics.

what's the BIG idea?

LINE GRAPHS

Line graphs are perfect for charting trends over a period of time. On these graphs, individual data points are plotted and straight lines are drawn between them. In this way we can see how something—perhaps the weather—changes over days or weeks.

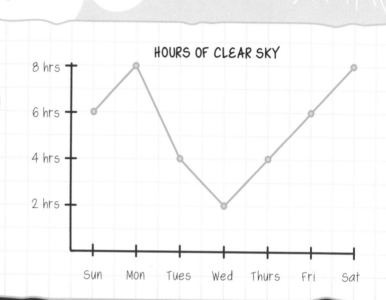

HOURS OF CLEAR SKY

WHAT'S GOING ON?

BAR CHARTS

In bar charts, the height of the bars show how often something happened—the frequency. For instance, it could show how many people gave a particular answer in a **survey**. Each bar represents a different **category**.

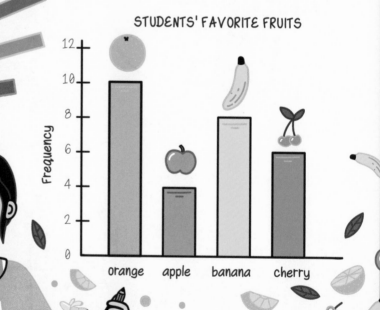

STUDENTS' FAVORITE FRUITS

what's the BIG idea?

PIE CHARTS

A pie chart shows how a whole group is divided into sections—each section gets its own slice of the circle depending on how much it contributes to the whole group.

reptiles 380 (7%)
mammals 430 (8%)
amphibians 400 (7%)
fish 3,000 (54%)
birds 1,300 (24%)

WHO WAS PLAYFAIR?

William Playfair (1759–1823) was a Scottish **engineer** who invented line graphs, bar charts, and pie charts as ways to show data.

TRY THIS AT HOME

PETS PIE CHART

Let's draw a pie chart to represent the following data about people's favorite pets.

360 people were asked which animal they would most like as a pet. Here's what the survey found:

Dogs — 165
Cats — 115
Rabbits — 55
Guinea Pigs — 15
Birds — 10

YOU WILL NEED:

- ✔ A protractor
- ✔ A compass (or something round to trace)
- ✔ A pencil
- ✔ A ruler
- ✔ Colored pencils

1 Because 360 people were surveyed, each person will be represented by one degree of the circle.

2 Draw a circle with a compass or trace a round object. Mark a dot on the edge of the circle at the top.

3 Use your protractor to measure out 165° from this dot, and mark a new dot.

4 Connect both of these dots to the center of the circle by drawing lines with a ruler.

5 Color in the segment you've made, and label it "Dogs."

6 Repeat this with the different quantities until you have completed the pie chart.

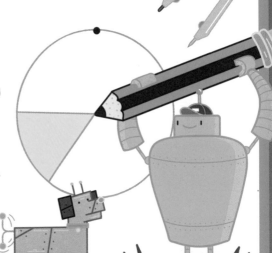

ANSWERS ARE AT THE BACK OF THE BOOK

Venn Diagrams and Set Theory

As a person, you belong to many groups. You are part of a family, a school, and perhaps a sports club. Similarly, mathematicians divide objects and numbers into groups called sets.

what's the BIG idea?

SET THEORY

We use curly brackets to indicate a set. For instance, let's look at the set "Vegetables." You could write Vegetables= {broccoli, carrots, potatoes, lettuce, ...}. Notice you normally write the individual members of the set in lowercase letters.

WHO WAS CANTOR?

Georg Cantor (1845–1918) was a German mathematician who invented the idea of sets—one of the most important areas in mathematics.

WHAT'S GOING ON?

VENN DIAGRAMS

Venn diagrams are a handy way to show sets. First you draw a rectangle. This is called the universe—every item will exist somewhere inside this rectangle. Then draw two or more overlapping circles. Each circle represents a set. If an item belongs in more than one set, it ends up in the intersection—the place where the circles overlap.

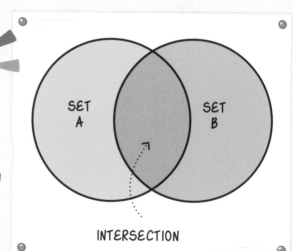

SET A

SET B

INTERSECTION

IN FACT...
CURLY BRACKETS

You can write the intersection of Set A and Set B as $A \cap B = \{..., ...\}$. You'd fill the curly brackets with all the items that appear in both sets.

WHO WAS VENN?

John Venn (1834–1923) was an English philosopher who invented the Venn diagram based on a similar diagram by Swiss mathematician Leonhard Euler.

TRY THIS AT HOME

AMPHIBIOUS ANIMALS

You're going to use your knowledge of animals to draw a Venn diagram.

YOU WILL NEED:

✔ A pencil
✔ Something circular to trace

1. Create a Venn diagram by drawing two overlapping circles as shown.

2. Label the left-hand circle "Land."

3. Label the right-hand circle "Water."

4. Can you think of animals that only belong in one of the circles? What about the other circle? Write them in.

5. Can you think of any animals that belong in the intersection—those that can live both on land and in water? How many can you think of? Write them in.

LAND   WATER

6. Write down the intersection in mathematical notation (see IN FACT... Curly Brackets, above).

7. Can you think of any animals that don't belong in either set? Write them outside the circles.

ANSWERS ARE AT THE BACK OF THE BOOK

AVERAGES

Averages are all about trying to find the middle and comparing different groups. If you're getting above average grades then you're doing better than most. If the number of games a sports team is winning is below average then they're doing worse than most.

what's the BIG idea?

MEAN, MEDIAN, MODE

There are three main types of averages, and they all begin with M! The most widely used is the mean. To find the mean value of a list of numbers, you simply add them all up and divide that total by how many numbers are in the list.

The median is calculated by re-arranging all the numbers from smallest to biggest and finding the number that sits right in the middle of the list.

The most common number in a list of data is called the mode.

AVERAGE BUILDING HEIGHTS

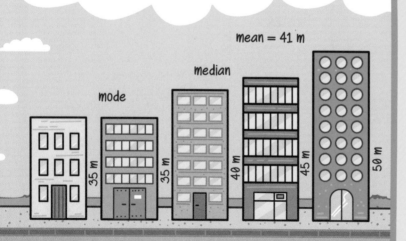

mean = 41 m

median

mode

35 m 35 m 40 m 45 m 50 m

WATCH OUT FOR OUTLIERS

31, 36, 34, 31,
42, 41, 40, 45
49, 39, <u>978</u>

There are times when it pays to use one measure of average over another. This is particularly true when dealing with outliers—very small or very big numbers compared to the other numbers in the list. They can skew the mean higher or lower, but have less of an effect on the median.

PUZZLE ZONE

AVERAGES AT THE OLYMPICS

Averages are used in gymnastic events at the Olympic Games. Five judges each give a gymnast a score for how well he/she has performed his/her routine (called an execution score). The highest and lowest scores are removed and the remaining three values are averaged (using the mean). This number is added to a score for the difficulty of the routine to give a final score for each gymnast.

Here are the execution and difficulty scores for three gymnasts. Can you figure out who wins the gold, silver and bronze medals?

GYMNAST 1
Difficulty Score: 5.7
Execution Scores:
6.5, 7.0, 7.5, 7.0, 6.0

GYMNAST 2
Difficulty Score: 6.0
Execution Scores:
7.5, 8.0, 7.5, 7.5, 7.0

GYMNAST 3
Difficulty Score: 5.2
Execution Scores:
8.5, 9.0, 9.5, 8.0, 9.0

KNOW YOUR DATA

Data can be about how well you are doing at school, the performance of your favorite sports team, or how much data you have left on your smartphone.

what's the BIG idea?

QUALITATIVE versus QUANTITATIVE

Data can be split into two main groups. Qualitative data describe things you cannot count: likes, feelings, opinions, decisions. Quantitative data describe things you can measure: height, distance, shoe size, exam scores.

feelings

shoe size

height

decisions

distance

opinions

likes

exam scores

QUALITATIVE DATA

QUANTITATIVE DATA

IN FACT...

DISCRETE VS. CONTINUOUS

There is another way to divide data into two groups. Discrete data can only take a limited number of values. Think clothing or shoe sizes. There is no size 10.31246. Continuous data can take any value; for example, height, time or weight.

WHAT'S GOING ON?

INTERPRETING DATA

A list of numbers about a particular topic isn't always useful on its own. You need to interpret the data—figure out what it is telling you. There are many ways to do this. You could create some **statistics** about the data—such as figuring out the mean, median, or mode (see p. 58). Or you could make an infographic of the data so it's clear for people to understand.

what's the BIG idea?

BIG DATA

The idea of "Big Data" is very popular. All the connected devices we use, such as smartphones and tablets, are constantly collecting data that companies keep in big databases. By analyzing all our data as one, it is possible to discover trends and patterns in human behavior.

PUZZLE ZONE

DATA SCALES

Take a look at this scale and the weights with data written on them. If you placed all the blocks labeled with quantitative data on the left-hand side of the scales, and placed the blocks labeled with qualitative data on the right-hand side, which way would the scales tip?

favorite ice creams

finger lengths

fastest 100 m sprints

number of sandwiches

sandwich fillings

heights of famous buildings

the weather

amount of rainfall

hair colors

shoe sizes

moods

ANSWERS ARE AT THE BACK OF THE BOOK

PROBABILITY

What are the chances of it raining tomorrow? How likely is it that your favorite music artist will make it to the Number 1 spot in the charts next week? Words like "chance" and "likely" are connected to probability.

what's the BIG idea?

IMPOSSIBLE TO CERTAIN

The chances of an event happening can range from impossible to certain, or somewhere in between. Mathematicians write probabilities as a number between 0 and 1. Something that's impossible has zero chance of happening. An event with a probability of 1 is guaranteed to happen.

IN FACT...

OTHER WAYS TO WRITE PROBABILITIES

You can also write probabilities as fractions and percentages. A probability of $0.25 = \frac{1}{4}$ or a 25% chance.

WHAT'S GOING ON?

MULTIPLE EVENTS

To combine probabilities of individual events together, you use the and/or rule. If you are looking for the chances of A happening and B also happening, you multiply the individual probabilities together. So the chances of you tossing two tails in a row is $\frac{1}{2} \times \frac{1}{2} = \frac{1}{4}$. (When you toss a coin, there are two possible outcomes, heads or tails.)

If you want to know the probability of A happening or B happening, you add the probabilities together. So the chances of tossing a heads or a tail $= \frac{1}{2} + \frac{1}{2} = 1$. Because there are no other options, it is certain you'll toss one or the other.

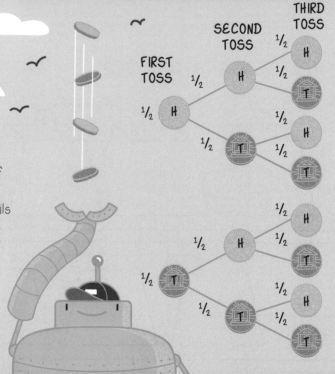

ROLLING A DIE

Dice are a great way to learn probabilities. In this activity you are going to make predictions about three questions and then perform an experiment to see if you were correct.

YOU WILL NEED:

- ✔ A die
- ✔ Paper
- ✔ A pencil

1 Think about the following three outcomes, and use what you've learned about probability to figure out the chances of them happening on a single roll:
- Rolling a six
- Rolling an even number
- Rolling a number beginning with the letter F

2 How many times would you expect these events to happen if you rolled the die fifty times?

Rolling a six	Rolling an even number	Rolling a number beginning with F

3 Roll the die fifty times and keep a tally chart, adding a mark each time one of these events occurs (don't forget one roll could check more than one box).

4 Compare your findings to your predictions at the beginning.

ANSWERS ARE AT THE BACK OF THE BOOK

HOW DOES IT WORK?

Even if you did the math correctly, you might not have gotten exactly the same outcome when you rolled. However, the more times you roll the die, the closer and closer you'll get to the expected probability.

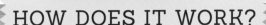

RATIONAL AND IRRATIONAL NUMBERS

Numbers that can be written as fractions are called rational numbers, and those that can't are called irrational numbers. Mathematicians, let's investigate!

what's the BIG idea?

RATIONALITY

The number 2.5 is a rational number because you can write it as $10 \div 4$. But what about pi (π)—the ratio of a circle's circumference to its diameter (see p. 30). You can write down fractions that come close to pi such as $^{22}/_7$ or $^{355}/_{113}$ but there is no fraction that will give you all of pi's digits. That's why it's an example of an irrational number.

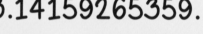

3.14159265359...

TRY THIS AT HOME

PROVING PI

No matter what circle you use, you'll always get the number pi (π). Here's a simple activity you can do to prove it:

YOU WILL NEED:

- ✔ A few circular household objects
- ✔ String
- ✔ Scissors
- ✔ A pen and paper
- ✔ Tape
- ✔ A ruler

1 Carefully wrap string around the circumference of your circular object.

2 Cut the string when it is exactly the same length as the circumference.

3 Take your "string circumference" and stretch it across the diameter of your circular object.

4 Cut as many "string diameters" from your "string circumference" as you can.

5 How many diameters could you cut? Write the number down.

6 Repeat steps 1-5 with other circular objects and compare your results. What do you notice?

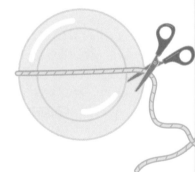

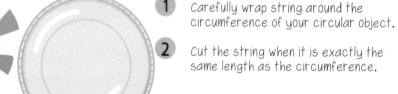

ANCIENT MYSTERY

In ancient Greece, many mathematicians believed that all numbers were rational and could be easily written as fractions. Legend has it that when the mathematician Hippasus discovered that some numbers were irrational, he drowned at sea under suspicious circumstances!

PUZZLE ZONE

CUTTING UP NUMBERS

Here's a puzzle for you to figure out. Take the number 40. Your job is to divide this number into equal parts, and then multiply those parts together to get the largest number you possibly can.

For example, you could divide it into 4 equal parts to give 10 x 10 x 10 x 10 = 10,000. Use the method of trial and error to see if you can get a higher answer by splitting it into a different number of equal parts. What's the highest you can get?

WHAT'S GOING ON?

THE GOLDEN RATIO

Another example of an irrational number is something called the Golden Ratio or phi φ. This number is approximately equal to 1.618. Two numbers are in the Golden Ratio if their ratio is the same as the ratio of them added together to the larger of the two quantities. In other words: You can find the Golden Ratio if you divide a line into two parts so the whole length divided by the long part is also equal to the long part divided by the short part.

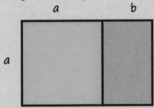

$$a + b \div a = a \div b = 1.618$$

You can keep dividing a Golden Ratio rectangle into a smaller square and rectangle that contains the same Golden Ratio. If you draw a curve through opposite corners of each of the squares, you create a spiral that looks like a snail's shell.

The Golden Ratio is linked to a number sequence known as the Fibonacci Sequence (see p. 18). Each number in the Fibonacci Sequence is equal to the two previous numbers added together. If you divide any number in the sequence by the one before, the result is a number close to 1.618. You can find this number pattern in nature—in the petals on flowers and on the branches of trees. In some sunflower heads, the seeds are set out as two spirals, turning in opposite directions. The number of spirals is a Fibonacci number.

55 counterclockwise spirals (55 is the 10th Fibonacci number in the sequence)

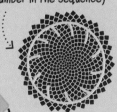

34 clockwise spirals (34 is the 9th Fibonacci number in the sequence)

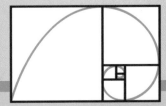

$$55 \div 34 = 1.618$$

MATH AS A LANGUAGE

In many ways, we can think of math as a language. It is the organizing language and the base of all others, from texting and emojis to all global languages.

$$^4/_{16} = {}^2/_8 = {}^1/_4$$

$$a^2 + b^2 = c^2$$

what's the BIG idea?

UNDERSTOOD BY ALL

Math is used everywhere. Imagine four mathematicians in a room—they are Japanese, Nigerian, Indian, and Canadian. They all speak and write in different languages from their regions, but if they wrote in math equations on a board, then they'd all understand the concepts, even if characters are used instead of alphabets. The various symbols for 4 all mean 4 in the same way to each person. You can think of an equation as the equivalent of a sentence—a sentence written not just with letter symbols, but with digit symbols, too.

IN FACT...

LANGUAGE ORDER

Some languages are written left to right (such as English), others right to left (such as Arabic), and some read top to bottom (such as Korean). But even if a mathematician writes his/her native language right to left, he/she will still write mathematical sentences left to right.

WHAT'S GOING ON?

TRANSLATION

Let's imagine you come across something written in another language. You need to translate it to understand it. Equally, if you come across a problem written in words, then sometimes you have to translate it into the language of mathematics to solve it. For example: "The length of a sports field is twice its width. The perimeter (see p. 32) is 300 m. What are its dimensions?" To find the answer, we need to translate this sentence of words into a mathematical sentence, or equation.

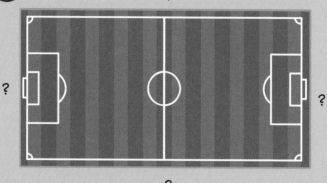

We could write: L = 2W and 2L + 2W = 300

We can substitute the first equation into the second to give 2L + L = 300 = 3L. That means L must be 100. If L is 100, then W must be half of that, or 50.

LETTERS IN MATH SENTENCES

We've seen that the letters x, y, or z can be used to represent numbers in problems, graphs, angles, and trigonometry. Letters are also used to write mathematical equations and sentences in algebra (see p. 70.) Because math is the base language that everyone can understand, and numbers are easier to translate as number symbols than as words, it is a good global language for people who make and trade things. It even provides its own way to translate itself if one country uses metric measurements and another uses imperial measuring systems. Let's imagine a pillow-making factory....

These robots make special pillows for people who have **allergies** and other medical problems. The pillow company uses robots rather than people to make the pillows because it's cheaper, can be germ-free, and they can get affordable and safe pillows to more people.

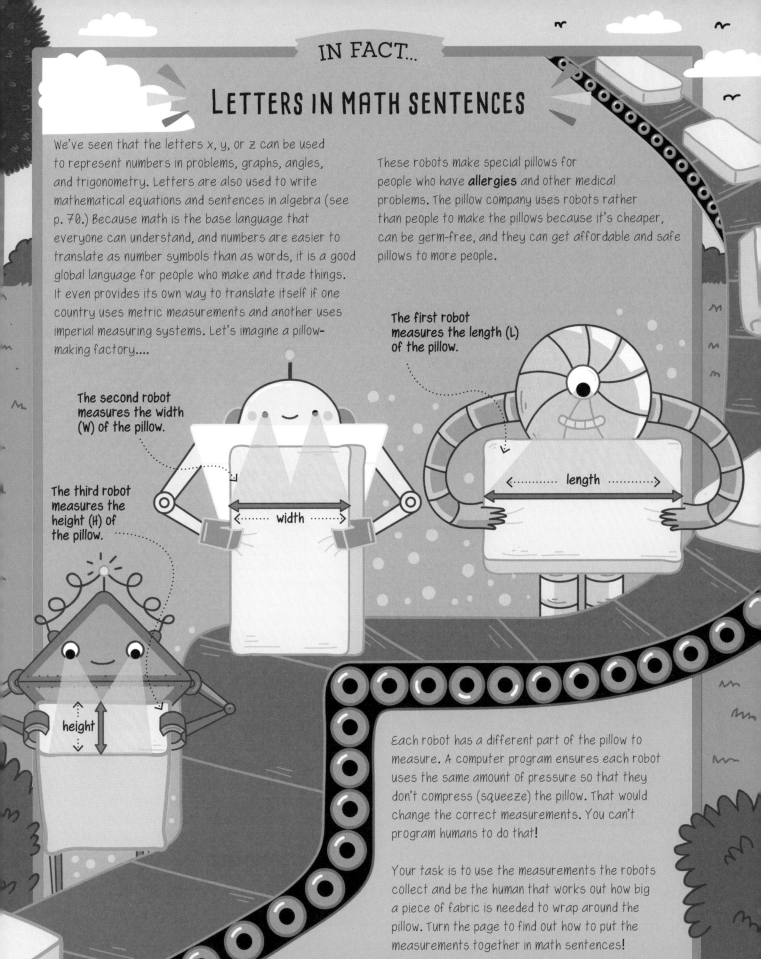

The first robot measures the length (L) of the pillow.

The second robot measures the width (W) of the pillow.

The third robot measures the height (H) of the pillow.

width

length

height

Each robot has a different part of the pillow to measure. A computer program ensures each robot uses the same amount of pressure so that they don't compress (squeeze) the pillow. That would change the correct measurements. You can't program humans to do that!

Your task is to use the measurements the robots collect and be the human that works out how big a piece of fabric is needed to wrap around the pillow. Turn the page to find out how to put the measurements together in math sentences!

FUNCTIONS

In math, functions are a way of turning one set of numbers into another. Think of them as little number factories producing outputs from inputs. There is one output for every input.

WRITING DOWN FUNCTIONS

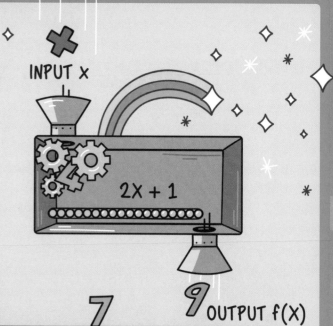

INPUT x

2X + 1

OUTPUT f(x)

Functions are often written as $f(x) =$. For example, it could be $f(x) = 2x + 1$. The function has a different output for each different input of x. Here x is called the **variable**. If a function depends on more than one variable, you should always include that on the left-hand side of the equal sign. For example $f(x,y) = 2x + 3y$.

FUNCTIONS IN COMPUTER PROGRAMMING

Writing computer code is a great skill to have, and it is important for many jobs both today and in the future. Functions are a big part of coding and the principle is the same —the code you write takes an input and turns it into a useful output.

```
<NAV>
  <UL>
    <LI><A HREF="#">Home</A></LI>
    <LI><A HREF="#">About</A></LI>
    <LI><A HREF="#">Clients</A></LI>
    <LI><A HREF="#">Contact Us</A></LI>
  </UL>
</NAV>
```

ROBOT PILLOW CHALLENGE

Let's go back to our busy robots working in the pillow factory on p. 67. See if you can figure out the measurements for pillows using math language.

NEED TO KNOW:

- To calculate the amount of fabric you'll need for the pillow, you need to think about the length (L), width (W), and height (H) of the pillow.

- A pillow can be made from one piece of fabric folded from the top, bottom, sides, and ends of the pillow, and then stitched together.

- If you unfold a pillow to see the shape of the fabric, you can do it in a variety of ways, but no matter which way you do it, you have one length (L) plus one end (N) or height, plus another length (L) and the other end (N) and two sides (S).

- To make it easier to cut the fabric and save time, Instead of cutting one side up and one side down, each side gets ½ the amount, and the middle (where the end is) is cut on an X. The stitching goes up the middle side of the pillow.

- Your pillow shouldn't be exactly the same size as the stuffing or it will be too tight and will rip. Add an extra 1 cm of fabric or "ease" (Z) to your length and width measurement.

- You also need to include **seam allowance** (M)—an extra area of fabric around the stitches (that secure the pieces of fabric together) so they do not fall out and unravel. Make this 1 cm all around your pillow outline.

Length = L (20 cm) Width = W (12 cm)
End (Height) = N (2 cm) Side = S (2 cm)
Ease = Z (2 cm) Seam allowance = M (1 cm)

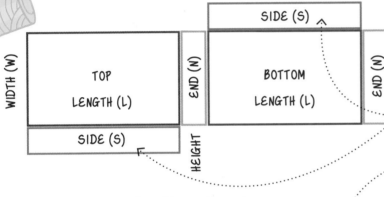

The fabric needed is the overall length x overall width:

Overall Length = 2L + 2N + 1Z + 2M

Overall Width = 1W + 1S + 1Z + 2M

Can you figure out how much fabric you'll need in total?

ANSWERS ARE AT THE BACK OF THE BOOK

ALGEBRA AND FORMULAS

Algebra is about using letters in mathematical sentences to represent numbers that we don't know the value of.

USING LETTERS

We use letters to represent unknown numbers, but why don't we just leave an empty space instead? Well, what if there are two unknown numbers you want to find? If you left an empty space you might get confused and think you were looking for the same number twice. It is much better to write $x + y + 3 = 6$ and figure out the values of x and y, and then replace letters with numbers.

WHAT'S GOING ON?

VARIABLES

$0.50

$0.75

You can also use letters in place of variables (quantities that can change). Let's say you've set up a stand selling lemonade and hot dogs. You sell lemonade for 50 cents and hot dogs for 75 cents. You can write a formula (rule) that tells you how much money you have received, such as $0.5L + 0.75H = M$. You might sell different amounts on different days, but by putting the number of sales of each item in place of L (lemonade) and H (hot dogs) you'll always get M—the total amount of money you received.

$$0.5L + 0.75H = M$$
or $0.5 \times 4 + 0.75 \times 7 = \$7.25$

SOLVING ALGEBRAIC PROBLEMS

How do you find the unknown number represented by a letter? One way is by taking it apart. You can perform a mathematical operation (adding, subtracting, multiplying, and dividing) to both sides of the equation. Let's say $x + 8 = 12$.

To find x you do the opposite of what the equation is doing, which is adding 8.

You subtract 8 from the left-hand side of the equation. But you must always do the same to the other side. So we end up with:
$x + 8 - 8 = 12 - 8$ or $x = 12 - 8$
So $x = 4$.

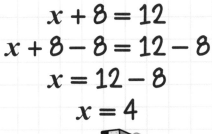

$$x + 8 = 12$$
$$x + 8 - 8 = 12 - 8$$
$$x = 12 - 8$$
$$x = 4$$

TRY THIS AT HOME

PERFECT SQUARE DETECTOR

In this activity you are going to use the Pythagorean Theorem to help you find out whether the corners of things around you are true squares.

YOU WILL NEED

☑ Things around you that look like they have square corners—tables, books, rooms, etc.

☑ A ruler

☑ A pencil

☑ Paper

☑ A cardboard box

☑ Tape

☑ A piece of paper larger than the cardboard box

NEED TO KNOW:

The formula $A^2 + B^2 = C^2$ will tell you if a corner is square—whether it is a right angle (90°).

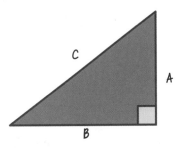

1 Measure the A, B, and C lengths (two sides and diagonal line) of the objects. Make a note of the measurements on the paper.

2 Next, follow the equation by checking if the sides A (squared) and B (squared) of an object added together equal the C diagonal (squared).

3 If it does, you know that the corner of your object is square (90°).

4 Now experiment by taking a cardboard box and removing the bottom. Tape the sides of the box to a large sheet of paper. Measure the sides and diagonal, and use the formula to check if the corners are square.

5 Repeat step 4. This time, squeeze the sides of the box so that the corners don't look like squares. Measure the sides and diagonal again, and use the formula to check whether the corners are square or not.

BINARY AND COMPUTING

Imagine the world without computers. So much of our lives are based around these machines that we'd be lost without them.

 what's the **BIG** idea ?

BINARY

Computers count differently than humans. Our number system (or **base**) uses 10 digits (0–9), but a computer only uses two—0 and 1. These are called binary digits (or bits). Counting in binary starts the same: 0 (for an "off" signal) then 1 (for an "on" signal), but what happens when you get to 2? You start again.

Base 10 system

10^4	10^3	10^2	10^1	10^0
10,000	1,000	100	10	1
0	0	0	5	9

$$5 \times 10 + 9 \times 1 = 59$$

Binary system

2^5	2^4	2^3	2^2	2^1	2^0
32	16	8	4	2	1
1	1	1	0	1	1

$$(1 \times 32) + (1 \times 16) + (1 \times 8) + (1 \times 2) + (1 \times 1) = 59$$

BASE 10 COUNTING	BINARY BASE COUNTING
0	0
1	1
2	10
3	11
4	100
5	101
6	110

WHO WAS BOOLE?

George Boole (1815–1864) was an English mathematician who created the rules for doing algebra with binary digits.

IN FACT...

BITS AND BYTES

Computers store information as bits (binary digits). There are eight bits to a byte. Then there are a million bytes to a megabyte, a billion in a gigabyte, and a trillion in a petabyte.

1 BIT

| 0 | 1 | 0 | 0 | 0 | 0 | 0 | 1 |

8 BITS = 1 BYTE

WHO WAS LOVELACE?

Ada Lovelace (1815–1852) was an English mathematician who is widely recognized as the world's first computer programmer.

TRY THIS AT HOME

EXPLORING BINARY

In this activity you're going to spell your name in the language of computers—binary code.

YOU WILL NEED:

✔ A pen ✔ Paper

1 Study this table of a basic computer code known as ASCII code.

2 Now take a look at how the binary code breaks down into binary counting.

3 Write a 9-column grid similar to this, but add a new row for each letter of your name. Did you manage to spell out your name in computer code?

LETTER	BINARY CODE
A	01000001
B	01000010
C	01000011
D	01000100
E	01000101
F	01000110
G	01000111
H	01001000
I	01001001
J	01001010
K	01001011
L	01001100
M	01001101
N	01001110
O	01001111
P	01010000
Q	01010001
R	01010010
S	01010011
T	01010100
U	01010101
V	01010110
W	01010111
X	01011000
Y	01011001
Z	01011010

	128	64	32	16	8	4	2	1
A	0	1	0	0	0	0	0	1

(1 X 64) +   (1 X 1) = 65

REASONING AND PROOFS

In everyday life, it may be difficult to prove something to be true beyond doubt. The beauty of mathematics is that you can use reasoning to construct solid mathematical proof.

what's the BIG idea?

CONSTRUCTING A PROOF

Take any whole number, square it, and subtract your original number. You'll notice that the answer is always even. But can you prove that's the case for all possible numbers without having to try every possibility?

Well, let's say you start with any even number. Squaring an even number always gives another even number. If you then take an even number away from that even number, your answer will always be even. So for any even starting number, we can prove the answer will always be even.

$$8^2 = 64$$
$$64 - 8 = 56$$

What about **odd numbers**? Squaring an odd number results in another odd number. Subtract one odd number from another and the answer is always even. All odd starting numbers must give even answers, too. Because all numbers are either even or odd, all starting numbers must give even answers.

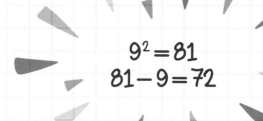

$$9^2 = 81$$
$$81 - 9 = 72$$

Therefore, we use logical reasoning and deduction to prove the rule holds for all numbers.

IN FACT...

INFINITE PRIMES

One of the most famous mathematical proofs was produced by the ancient Greek mathematician Euclid. He was able to show that the list of primes (see p. 14) is infinite—that is, it just goes on forever without any limit.

FERMAT'S LAST THEOREM

We know from the Pythagorean Theorem (see p. 38) that for right triangles $a^2 + b^2 = c^2$, but what about the more general equation $a^n + b^n = c^n$? Here, n can be any whole number and a, b, and c are three different numbers. French mathematician Pierre de Fermat (1607–1665) predicted in 1637 that when n is more than two, there are no values for a, b, and c that make the equation work. But it took until 1994 for English mathematician Andrew Wiles to provide a proof that Fermat was right.

PUZZLE ZONE

DETECTIVE CHALLENGE

When you use reason to solve something, you are acting like a detective. **Logic** and reasoning is used to prove many things in real life—for instance, in court, in science, in figuring out how much to pay for something, or even in guessing what will happen in a movie. We use logic all the time. But sometimes a puzzle is too hard to solve in your head. So you write down the clues and make charts or math maps to figure it out.

Look at the chart below. By studying the hints, can you figure out who wants to have what career based on which summer camp each student chose? Copy the chart and write an x where you've figured out the careers or camps that don't apply to each student, and a check for the camps or careers that do apply.

HINTS:

- 3 students are interested in going to a Music, Sports, or Gaming summer camp.

- One student wishes to be a scientist, one an engineer, and one a mathematician.

- Mary wants to be a scientist.

- Casey did not choose gaming camp.

- The student who wanted to be an engineer chose music camp.

- The student who chose sports camp does not want to become a scientist.

- Casey is a master at solving algebra equations.

	MARY	ROBIN	CASEY
Scientist	√	X	X
Engineer	X		
Mathematician	X		
Music Camp			
Gaming Camp			
Sports Camp			

Glossary

ALGEBRA
A branch of math that uses letters or other symbols to stand for numbers.

ALLERGIES
A physical reaction to something, such as a type of food, that doesn't usually cause a problem for people.

BASE
The number on which a counting system is based. Our counting system is base 10: after counting to 9, we add another digit and reuse figures, starting 10, 11, 12, and so on.

CATEGORY
A group of similar objects when things are being organized. For example, we could group animals into categories, such as birds, mammals, fish, and reptiles.

CURRENCY
A system of units of money. Different countries have different currencies.

DAM
A structure built across a river to stop or control the flow of water.

DATA
A collection of information, such as a list of people's heights or the names of everyone who live on a street.

DIGIT
A single-figure number: 0, 1, 2, 3, 4, 5, 6, 7, 8, or 9.

DIMENSIONAL
Relating to the number of dimensions (or lengths) something occupies: A line has one dimension, area has two dimensions, and a solid shape or volume has three dimensions.

ENGINEER
A person who designs and builds equipment, machines, and structures and keeps them in good condition.

EQUATION
A mathematical sentence showing that two statements have the same value. For example, $2 + 3 = 6 - 1$.

EVEN NUMBER
A number that is exactly divisible by 2, such as 4, 8, or 10.

EXPONENT
The power to which a number is raised is the number of times it must be multiplied by itself. For example, in 2^4 the exponent is 4, so 2 must be multiplied by itself 4 times: $2 \times 2 \times 2 \times 2$.

FORESTRY
The planting and caring for trees in forests.

FORMULA
A mathematical "recipe" or rule for calculating something. For example, the formula width x height = area tells you how to figure out the area of a rectangle.

GEOMETRY
A branch of mathematics that uses points, lines, angles, and shapes.

LOGIC
Using reasoning and careful thought to understand something or to solve a problem.

ODD NUMBER
A number that is not divisible by 2, such as 5, 7, or 9.

ORIENTATION
The angle at which an object is positioned compared to the axes of a graph.

PHILOSOPHER
A person who tries to solve problems through thought and reason. A philosopher often tackles questions that can't be solved by scientific investigation, such as "are some actions always bad?" or "should animals have rights?"

PHONE TOWER
A tall structure, such as a mast or a tower, used to pick up and send phone signals.

PHYSICS
The scientific study of energy and forces.

RESERVOIR
A large body of stored water, often in a vast outdoor, open tank.

ROMAN NUMERALS
System of writing numbers used by the ancient Romans. Numbers were built by arranging and repeating letters that stood for units (I), tens (X), hundreds (C), and so on.

SEAM ALLOWANCE
The area between a line of stitches in a seam and the edge of a piece of fabric.

STATISTICS

A branch of mathematics that uses number data, such as measurements and quantities, to explore the world.

SURVEY

A method of investigating by asking people questions or making measurements, then using the results to draw conclusions. For example, a survey about pets might ask all children in a class what types of pet they have to discover the most common type.

SURVEYING

Making scientific surveys of the land.

UNIT OF MEASUREMENT

A set quantity of something that is accepted as a standard measurement, such as a meter, foot, or dollar.

VARIABLE

A quantity in a mathematical sentence that can change. For example, the diameter of a circle is 2 x radius, and this is true for any value of the variable "radius."

WIND TURBINE

A machine with turning blades that uses the power of the wind to generate electricity.

ANSWERS

PAGES 8-9 ADDING AND SUBTRACTING

Calculator sums

107 + 282 + 215 = HOG

88 + 161 + 89 = BEE

27432 + 7574 = GOOSE

199 + 198 + 197 + 139 = EEL

PAGES 10-11 MULTIPLYING AND DIVIDING

Palindromic multiplication

Palindrome numbers are:

143 x 7 = 1001

407 X 3 = 1221

33 X 11 = 363

PAGES 14-15 PRIME NUMBERS AND POWERS

Prime numbers up to 50

Prime numbers are: 2, 3, 5, 7, 11, 13, 17, 19, 23, 29, 31, 37, 41, 43, 47

PAGES 20-21 FABULOUS FRACTIONS

Fraction maze

The path through the maze is: $2/16$, $1/6$, $1/3$, $1/2$, $4/5$, $8/9$

PAGES 28-29 MONEY AND INTEREST

Playing with pennies

Bag 1 has one penny, bag 2 has two pennies, bag 3 has four pennies, and bag 4 has eight pennies. These are the bags you'd need if you wanted to pay each of the following values:

1 penny = bag 1

2 pennies = bag 2

3 pennies = bag 2 + bag 1

4 pennies = bag 3

5 pennies = bag 1 + bag 3

6 pennies = bag 2 + bag 3

7 pennies = bag 1 + bag 2 + bag 3

8 pennies = bag 4

9 pennies = bag 1 + bag 4

10 pennies = bag 2 + bag 4

11 pennies = bag 4 + bag 2 + bag 1

12 pennies = bag 4 + bag 3

13 pennies = bag 4 + bag 3 + bag 1

14 pennies = bag 4 + bag 3 + bag 2

15 pennies = bag 4 + bag 3 + bag 2 + bag 1

Want it! Need it! Save for it!

If you put $500 into a bank account with an interest rate of 2.5% for 10 years, you would earn $125.00.

Robber riddle

The answer is $100. The thief ended up with $80 worth of merchandise and $20 of cash. Whatever the thief gained the owner lost.

PAGES 32-33 PERIMETER, AREA, AND VOLUME

How fast is the earth moving?

$(2 \times \pi \times R) \div 8766 = 107{,}228$ km/hr

Birthday cake

A circle would give you the biggest surface area.

PAGES 36-37 TERRIFIC TRIANGLES

Tricky triangles

The number of triangles is 35.

PAGES 38-39 PYTHAGOREAN THEOREM AND TRIGONOMETRY

Pythagorean Theorem in Practice

There are five dots on the longest side.

PAGES 40–41 2-D SHAPES

Amazing angles

There are always two fewer triangles than number of sides or n-2. The rule for working out the size of the angles is $((n-2) \times 180)/n$. So, 108° for a pentagon and 120° for a hexagon. A dodecagon can be split into ten triangles and an enneacontagon into 88.

PAGES 42–43 TESSELLATIONS

The semi-regular tessellations are:

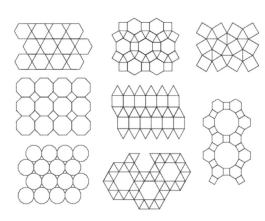

PAGES 48–49 TRANSFORMATIONS

Congruent shapes

The three congruent shapes are:

PAGES 52–53 COORDINATES

Hunt for the dinosaur egg

The egg is hidden at (10, 3). The correct coordinates are
4. (0,2), (3,4), (4,4), (5,3), (10,3).

PAGES 54–55 CHARTS AND GRAPHS

Pets pie chart

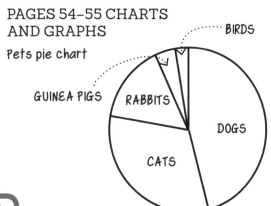

PAGES 56–57 VENN DIAGRAMS AND SET THEORY

Amphibious animals

Animals that belong in the intersection are amphibians, such as frogs, toads, salamanders, and caecilians. For example, Land ∩ Water = {frogs, toads, salamanders, caecilians}.

PAGES 58–59 AVERAGES

Averages at the Olympics

Gymnast 1 wins the bronze medal—12.5 points.

Gymnast 2 wins the silver medal—13.5 points.

Gymnast 3 wins the gold medal—14.0 points.

PAGES 60–61 KNOW YOUR DATA

Data scales

The scales would tip to the left.

PAGES 62–63 PROBABILITY

Rolling a die

The probability of rolling a six is $1/6$.

The probability of rolling an even number is $1/2$.

The probability of rolling a number beginning with the letter F is $2/6$ or $1/3$.

PAGES 64–65 RATIONAL AND IRRATIONAL NUMBERS

Cutting up numbers

1,202,604 (by splitting 40 into 14 parts each equal to a special irrational number called e = 2.718...)

PAGES 68–69 FUNCTIONS

Robot pillow challenge

Overall Length of Pillow = (2 x 20 = 40) + (2 x 2 = 4) + (1 x 2 = 2) + (2 x 1 = 2) = 48 cm

Overall Width of Pillow = (1 x 12 = 12) + (1 x 2 = 2) + (1 x 2 = 2) + (2 x 1 = 2) = 18 cm

PAGES 74–75 REASONING AND PROOFS

Detective challenge

Mary wants to be a scientist and chose a gaming camp. Robin wants to be an engineer and chose a music camp. Casey wants to be a mathematician and chose a sports camp.

INDEX

Index entries in **bold** refer to experiments and projects.